LOST HIGHWAY

THE FIST OF LOVE

WRITTEN BY SCOTT RYAN

SCOTT LUCK STORIES
(2014)
THIRTYSOMETHING AT THIRTY: AN ORAL HISTORY
(2017)
THE LAST DAYS OF LETTERMAN
(2019)
BUT, COULDN'T I DO THAT? ANSWERING YOUR QUESTIONS
ABOUT SELF-PUBLISHING (WITH ERIN O'NEIL)
(2021)
MOONLIGHTING: AN ORAL HISTORY
(2021)
FIRE WALK WITH ME:
YOUR LAURA DISAPPEARED
(2022)

EDITED BY SCOTT RYAN

THE BLUE ROSE MAGAZINE
(2017-CURRENT)
THE WOMEN OF DAVID LYNCH
(2019)
THE WOMEN OF AMY SHERMAN-PALLADINO
(2020)
TWIN PEAKS UNWRAPPED
(WRITTEN BY BEN DURANT & BRYON KOZACZKA)
(2020)
MASSILLON TIGERS: 15 FOR 15
(WRITTEN BY DAVID LEE MORGAN, JR.)
(2020)
MYTH OR MAYOR: THE SEARCH FOR MY FAMILY'S LEGACY
(WRITTEN BY ALEX RYAN/AFTERWORD BY SCOTT RYAN)
(2021)
BARBRA STREISAND: THE ALBUMS, THE SINGLES, THE MUSIC
(WRITTEN BY MATT HOWE)
(2023)

LOST HIGHWAY

THE FIST OF LOVE

Scott Ryan

TUCKER

DS

PRESS

Cover designs by Scott Ryan
Cover photos courtesy of Peter Deming
Back cover photos courtesy of Janus Films
Author photo by Faye Murman
All photos/captures from *Lost Highway* are courtesy of Ciby 2000/Criterion
All full page photos courtesy of Peter Deming except Jack Nance collage by Scott Ryan
Edited by Alex Ryan
Special Thanks to David Bushman
Book designed by Scott Ryan

Published in the USA by Tucker DS Press
Columbus, Ohio

Contact Information
Email: TuckerDSPress@gmail.com
Website: TuckerDSPress.com
Twitter: @FMPBooks
Instagram: @Fayettevillemafiapress
ISBN: 9781959748021
eBook ISBN: 9781959748038

For Alex Ryan

Who stopped me from watching *Lost Highway* in 1997
and then edited this book in 2022.

CONTENTS

"You said you loved me.
Or were you just being kind?
Or am I losing my mind?"
—Stephen Sondheim
"Losing My Mind," *Follies* (1971)

"You'll never have me."
—Alice
Lost Highway

FOREWORD

BY MATT ZOLLER SEITZ

David Lynch's *Lost Highway* could be a companion piece to a lot of great works in other media, but one that resonates especially strongly is Robert Frost's "The Road Not Taken," which ends with

> Two roads diverged in a wood, and I—
> I took the one less traveled by,
> And that has made all the difference.

This is the film where David Lynch's career took the road less traveled, and the filmmaker never looked back. In the time that has elapsed since its original release, we can see *Lost Highway*, an experimental neo-noir that loops back on itself like an ouroboros or Möbius strip, as the fork in the road of Lynch's identity as a filmmaker. Its release steered him away from the mainstream success that he'd inexplicably found between the mideighties and early nineties, and recommitted him fully to the unconscious and uncanny images he'd explored as an art school student and deepened as a creator of experimental fine art. Lynch's film and TV works after *Lost Highway* are intended to be looked at and reacted to, not "understood" in any conventional way, and certainly not "solved." They aren't puzzles or riddles, but works of personal expression. And they seem oblivious to viewers' desire to explain and "solve" everything that they consume. There are many theories about what "happens" in this film. None of them explain it because the film is not meant to be explained. It's meant to be absorbed, felt, and discussed.

Lost Highway is broken into halves and swaps leading men (from Bill Pullman to Balthazar Getty and back again) while keeping the same leading lady (Patricia Arquette) in each half. It ends with a sequence of shots that makes it seem as if the film could start again in the same place, and unfold in an endless, seamless loop until the end of time. One story is sort of a film noir murder mystery, about a saxophone player named Fred Madison (Pullman) whose homelife with his wife, the dark-haired beauty Renee (Arquette), is disrupted when somebody begins sending them invasive videotapes of their private lives, and a menacing figure known as the Mystery Man (Robert Blake) repeatedly appears to Fred in both "reality" and in his dreams. By the end, Fred is convinced (based on video "evidence") that he's murdered Renee and goes to jail for the crime, and is inexplicably replaced by Balthazar Getty's Pete Dayton, a mechanic who fixes cars for gang boss Mr. Eddy (Robert Loggia) and who ends up falling in love with Eddy's platinum blonde trophy girl Alice Wakefield (Arquette again) and getting into a standard-issue film noir plot to help her escape her brutal husband and start a new life.

Patricia Arquette and Bill Pullman in the first path before the road not taken jumps in. Photos courtesy of Janus Films

The movie doesn't judge anyone morally, but nevertheless there are intimations of purgatorial punishment attached to the characters' actions. They seem to be fated (or cursed) to do certain things and have certain things done to them as a result, or in response. Perhaps all of *Lost Highway*'s characters are doomed to live out this narrative loop, and maybe karma is involved—but whose karma is whose? Is one universe cause and the other effect? Or are they causing and affecting each other constantly—as suggested when both Fred and Pete see glimpses of life as the other man, and in the scene where Fred dreams of walls and corridors of red curtains that, when parted, unveil a different life, timeline, or plane of existence? Even this doesn't quite track, because Fred becomes Pete and then Pete becomes Fred in a single story loop, and it appears that Alice and Renee both exist within that loop. (Like so many Lynch films, this one is haunted by the aftertraces of Alfred Hitchcock's *Vertigo*, about a man who becomes fixated on transforming his new girlfriend into a replacement for an obsession object that he lost, unaware that the first woman was never actually lost, and that in fact they're the same person.)

Every attempt to pin *Lost Highway*'s meanings down to a fixed definition or interpretation is bound to end in failure because the entire construction is permeable on both narrative and symbolic levels, in a way that obliterates all rational thoughts that viewers try to apply to it. What is geography in this film? What is time? Fred sees Pete and Pete sees Fred and they both see visions of Alice and Renee and the Mystery Man. A house on struts is on fire, but the flames and smoke move backward, and later in the movie, you see it standing intact but about to explode (in one sense or another). The Mystery Man perhaps causes Fred to murder Renee (or entices him into it) or maybe he doesn't. When characters die in this film, is it in reaction to something that another iteration of their character did, and if so, which action is in the past and which is in the future? We don't know. We can't know. It's not that kind of movie.

Lynch burst onto screens with 1977's *Eraserhead*, a surrealism-inflected domestic horror movie that was plotted like a dream and packed with haunting and sometimes horrifying images, but was told in a more-or-less linear manner, and set in a universe whose dreamlike internal logic was not difficult to understand if the viewer resolved to commit to Lynch's unique vision. From *Dune* and *Blue Velvet* through *Wild at Heart* and its prequel film *Twin Peaks: Fire Walk With Me*, Lynch had always challenged (or provoked) his audiences by creating worlds that felt simultaneously modern and old, and that were perched on the edge of abstraction but never pitched themselves over the brink. After *Lost Highway*, Lynch made one fully rational and linear drama, *The Straight Story* (though with a slightly surreal flavor at times) and from there he did *Mulholland Dr.*, *Inland Empire*, and *Twin Peaks: The Return*, each more defiantly opaque yet engrossing than the one that came before. The work doesn't just loop back on itself and tear holes in itself so that you can see what's inside or outside, it disintegrates and re-integrates as you watch, and ends and begins itself repeatedly, and creates little interludes where narrative is meaningless and it's all about the experience of time passing, and thoughts passing through your mind, and before your eyes. Lynch chose this branch of the highway in 1996, and he's been on it ever since.

The chase begins and/or ends. Photo courtesy of Peter Deming

The new 4K restoration poster created for the summer of 2022 release. Photo courtesy of Janus Films

PROLOGUE: THE ON-RAMP

In discussing his film *Lost Highway* for a DVD release, David Lynch said, "I didn't ever say anything at the time, but I had a fixation on O. J. Simpson, the trial, and I think some of [*Lost Highway*] grew out of O. J. Simpson. Because here is a guy who, at least I believe, committed two murders, and yet is able to go on living, and speaking, and golfing. So what is in the mind? When after a horrific murder and that experience, how does the mind protect itself from that knowledge and go on? That's interesting to me and the mind is interesting for sure."

On October 3, 1995, more than 150 million viewers, 57 percent of the US, tuned in to watch the live broadcast of the O. J. Simpson verdict. When you take into account the above quote, David Lynch must certainly have been one of them. I was not. Most times when pop culture tells me to Macarena, I leave the dance floor immediately. I believe it's the Gen X in me. My peers raised me to believe that if everyone else likes it, then I shouldn't. I was also a huge David Letterman fan and while his competitor, The Mystery Man of late-night television Jay Leno, was covering the trial nonstop, Letterman was not mentioning the national obsession on his late-night show and told guest Howard Stern, "I guess I just don't find double homicide as amusing as I used to." America did, still does, and always will.

The good ol' US of A ate up that trial and every detail about a football player turned murderer like it was something that mattered. Since I never consumed any of the trial back in the nineties, I am often told that I should watch *this* documentary about the Simpson trial. I should read *that* book about it. I should watch *this* limited series about it. The common refrain is "you'll learn that the trial was about more than just a double homicide." I smile and lie, saying that I'll check it out, but I never will. I am not big on actual murder for entertainment. I do not do true crime because of the first word in the description. I just don't find real homicide as amusing as my country does. Instead, I tell them that *they* should check out *Lost Highway*. It's also about O. J., and they will learn something. As I walk away, I laugh as if I am Mr. Eddy leaving someone I caught tailgating. I know exactly what I did to them, and I feel no guilt about it. I wasn't the only one who wasn't amused by all that murder. David Lynch didn't find it amusing either. He found it baffling. And just like a truly great artist should, he took his bafflement and constructed one of his most challenging films. And in his filmography, that is really saying something.

Out of this national obsession, David Lynch went fishing in the pond of ideas and caught a new big idea. He would make a movie about the *idea* of what the mind must go through to convince itself that a murderer didn't do anything wrong. He conceived his film in a moment that over 150 million people were interested in and ended up making the lowest-grossing, most-forgotten film of his career. I have no firsthand knowledge of what effect that had on David Lynch. He would never talk about box office expectations with someone like me. Who am I kidding? He would never give an interview to an author like me. But I do know from the plethora of interviews he gave to major publications that he does worry about the number of people that consume his work. He told *Rolling Stone* magazine the year the film came out, "I hope it would be possible to make a film that has some depth to it but that still has a strong story and great characters, and that people would really appreciate." He reiterated his desire for the masses to love his work in his book with Kristine McKenna, *Room to Dream*, where he relayed a story about interacting with one of the most successful directors of all time, Steven Spielberg.

Lynch told Spielberg at a party, "You're so lucky because the things you love millions of people love, and the things I love thousands of people love." Spielberg replied, "David, we're getting to the point where just as many people will have seen *Eraserhead* as have seen *Jaws*."

David Lynch, like any artist, wants his work to be seen, but none of Lynch's films have truly rocked the box office *Jaws*-style. The fact that he got his initial idea from something that he *knew* everyone was watching and it still didn't light up the box office or the culture just had to sting. I submit that no film in Lynch's canon has been more forgotten than *Lost Highway*. Several of his films were released and were loudly hated, several were nominated for awards, and several were critical darlings, but only *Lost Highway* came out and was just ignored. For so many years, the film was lost itself. It was hard to find, and the existing versions were released with an extremely low quality. The picture was dark and blurry, and the sound was abysmal. All these qualities matter in a Lynch film more than most. Plus, no one was really screening the film in theaters outside of Lynch film fests that showed all of his work. Disagree that it's his most forgotten film? Here is a quick trip through his filmography up to 2023.

- 1977's *Eraserhead* became a midnight screening sensation that still plays around the globe at midnight. If it isn't the most popular student film of all time, it sure as heck is in the top two. (Gross: $7 million)

Lynch's second film was *The Elephant Man.*
Photo courtesy of Brooks Films

- 1980's *The Elephant Man* was nominated for numerous Oscars, including his first best director nomination, and put Lynch on the Hollywood map. The quote "I am not an animal" is ingrained in pop culture and was even quoted on an episode of *Seinfeld*. (Gross: $26 million)
- 1984's *Dune* was much maligned and taught Lynch that he must have final cut or there was no point in making a film. This was also his first time working with Kyle MacLachlan (*Dune, Blue Velvet, Twin Peaks*). Even though *Dune* was not embraced at the time, it is his highest-grossing film to date. (Gross: $30.9 million)
- 1986's *Blue Velvet* was a critical darling and certainly is seen as the film that cemented Lynch's legacy as one of the most idiosyncratic directors of his time. Oscars and critics came a calling with Lynch's second nomination for best director. This film brought him together with his lifelong muse, Laura Dern (*Blue Velvet, Wild at Heart, Inland Empire, Twin Peaks: The Return*). Film lovers never dismissed or forgot Dennis Hopper (Frank Booth) and his breathing mask. (Gross: $8.5 million)

Lynch and Dern work together for the first time in *Blue Velvet*.
Photo courtesy of De Laurentiis Entertainment Group

- 1990's *Wild at Heart* might not have been embraced in America, but it won the Palme d'Or award at the Cannes Film Festival and did well at the box office for an independent film. Critics were split on whether the film was a classic or classless, but everyone took a side, and that is better than being ignored. (Gross: $14.5 million)

- 1992's *Fire Walk With Me* was hated just about everywhere and in every way a film can be hated, but it certainly was not forgotten. *Twin Peaks* fans weren't going to allow that to happen. (I've even heard that there was a book written about this film for its thirtieth anniversary. But that can't be true, can it?) The film might have started at the bottom of the heap, but over the last thirty years it has risen to the top with critics and fans who finally came around to the story. I don't know the exact tally, but I wouldn't be surprised if this film has been released and repackaged more than *Jaws* has ever been. (Gross: $4 million)

- 1997's *Lost Highway* came and went in a videotaped blip. It performed even worse than *Fire Walk With Me*, and that was a film that was taken to the train car of hateful reviews. *Lost Highway* had a lackluster release on VHS with one of the worst transfers ever and didn't get a special edition release or restoration until 2022. Only the soundtrack made a splash, hitting number seven on the *Billboard* Hot 100 chart and achieving gold status. (Gross: $3.6 million)

- 1999's *The Straight Story* was released by Disney, and while by Disney standards it might not be remembered like *The Lion King*, Lynch did receive some of the best reviews of his career. Once again, Oscar took note with Richard Farnsworth receiving a nomination for lead actor. (Gross: $6.2 million)

- 2001's *Mulholland Dr.* needs no help from anyone in securing its legacy. It was picked as the best film of the new millennium by the United Kingdom newspaper *The Independent*. (And it had to compete with twelve Spiderman films and forty-eight Batman films, so that honor *really* means something.) The film brought Lynch another directing nomination and turned Naomi Watts into a megastar. (Gross: $7.2 million)

Laura Dern in *Inland Empire*
Photo courtesy of Janus Films

- 2006's *Inland Empire* might draw the best argument against my claim that *Lost Highway* is Lynch's most overlooked film, but if you think about the amount of gruff people gave *Inland Empire* for the poor quality of the digital film, that alone makes the film memorable. Now, add in the cow and Laura Dern incident (no, I won't explain what that means because it's fun to write that collection of words without explanation) along with the fact that *Inland Empire* had a 4K restoration before *Lost Highway* and there is enough evidence to push it past *Lost Highway*. Both films were rereleased in 2022 with new restorations. *Inland Empire* grossed an additional $200,000 plus and *Lost Highway* just $50,000 more—another win for *Inland Empire*. Finally, if you have ever met a Lynch fan who has sat through this three-hour movie, they will always wear that act like a badge of honor. They need to let you know that they have seen the film and that makes them better than you. (Gross: $4 million.)

Lost Highway is the lost Lynch film. One contributing factor is that it is a difficult film to comprehend on one viewing. If you haven't seen the film, I will do my best to explain the plot and the concept in Chapter Two, but for now, just understand that if you try to force the film to be like every other film you've ever seen, then you are never going to get it. Basically, you must be willing to put in a little bit of work to experience the film as Lynch intended. But honestly, not a ton of work. It's not like all the dialogue is written in iambic pentameter. There are clues given throughout the film. He helps you along; you just have to be open to it. That being said, the movie has some difficult scenes to watch. It can revolt the viewer if they are not ready or open to the ideas. To give you a bit of an example, I tried to do that in the beginning of this prologue.

If earlier in this essay your back stiffened and you got mad at me when I said I didn't watch the O. J. trial and the country shouldn't have been obsessed with it, don't be mad. I did it on purpose. I know an author isn't supposed to say, "OK, you all stand over there. I'm gonna be over here by myself on the moral high ground." (I'm not Obi-Wan Kenobi.) But I thought this was a great way to bring you into a David Lynch film. When he makes a piece of art, he doesn't care what you think about him. He stays true to the idea. He only cares about how to bring his idea to life in the most honest and raw way. If you base your film on something as dark and disturbing as a real-life killer who murders two people and then acts like he is innocent, well, that isn't going to be a very "fun" film to watch. This could be a reason why the film wasn't embraced in its time. *Lost Highway* is a difficult look at misogyny, murder, and schizophrenia. I mean, should there be a "fun" film that covers those topics? Television series like *Law & Order*, *Bones*, and *CSI* have trained us to believe that murder is just fine as long as we enjoy finding out who did it. It's OK to kill someone as long as the villain is punished and the hardworking detectives solve the crime while they also fall in love. But what if instead of the story focusing on the mystery of solving it, the story is a look at the inside of the mind that committed the brutal act? What if a film isn't plot based, but instead based on emotions and other intangibles? Well, probably that film would be a forgotten film that people would erroneously just dismiss as being too confusing.

When I interviewed Duwayne Dunham, the editor of several Lynch films (*Blue Velvet*, *Wild at Heart*), Dunham corroborated that Lynch doesn't talk in specifics when creating. Dunham told me, "David doesn't say, 'Cut here' or 'Cut there.' He would talk to me [about editing] like he would talk to Angelo Badalamenti, or to an actor. He would say, 'Make it more blue' or 'Make it more yellow.'" Whatever topic Lynch is covering in his work, be it parenting (*Eraserhead*), sexual abuse (*Fire Walk With Me*), or small-town America (*Blue Velvet*), he always tackles the topic with complete honesty and no filter. Plot is of no interest to Lynch. He does things by emotion. He doesn't mind showing audiences the inner workings of trauma, anger, or lust. In doing so, he ends up displaying the true meaning of love (*Wild at Heart*), humanity (*The Elephant Man*), and kindness (*The Straight Story*). In a piece of Lynch art, you can't have true goodness without true evil. Most of his films have both, but there really isn't any love in *Lost Highway*. It is heavy on darkness; this could be another reason why the film didn't have success. This idea that *Lost Highway* is a lost and forgotten film can be disagreed with, but one fact that can't be disputed is that *Lost Highway* is his lowest-grossing film, at $3.6 million. Yet, it was about a subject that everyone was interested in: O. J. Simpson. So why was it so ignored?

Alvin Straight finds kindness on a ride across the country in *The Straight Story*. Photo courtesy of Walt Disney Pictures

If you are a Lynch fan, you already know the answer to my long setup. Sorry for wasting your time. Go ahead and doom scroll on your phone to see if there are any new murder trials to follow while I bring this home. O. J. was just the *idea* that sparked Lynch. I mean, there isn't even a single dancing Ito in the entire film. The average moviegoer wouldn't really get that *Lost Highway* had a damn thing to do with the trial. They probably wouldn't get it even if you told them right before and after they viewed the film. The first time a moviegoer watches *Lost Highway*, that is not what they are going to focus on. They want to know where the hell the Bill Pullman character went, and whether Patricia Arquette is playing one character or two. They are not concerned about the feeling; they are focusing on the plot. And who could blame them? There are a lot of provocative scenes in the film that can distract a first-time viewer. The most honest thing Lynch ever told his fans was to keep your eye on the doughnut and not the hole.

Director David Lynch and screenwriters Barry Gifford and Lynch took this spark of an idea and crafted a complex, wonderful, lustful, misogynistic, beautiful, sexy, scary, funny, perplexing, colorful, dark, cacophony of horrible and glorious sounds, all stitched together by the most Lynchian elements that fans of his work should have devoured as quickly as the mechanical shark devoured Quint's boat in *Jaws*.

Well, with all this praise from me, I must have, of course, loved *Lost Highway* the first time I ever saw it, right? Wrong. The first time I saw it, I pushed stop and ejected the VHS tape, popped it back into its rental case at exactly 7:29 minutes into the film, and didn't watch it again for twenty years. So, naturally, I am doing an entire book on it.

Welcome to *Lost Highway: The Fist of Love*.

CHAPTER 1
I'M DERANGED

In January 1997, I became the father of twins. I was a full-time stay-at-home dad and the primary caregiver to two human beings. I lived in a continuous time loop. The twins ate every three hours. It took about an hour to feed, change, and then put them back to bed. That left only two hours to sleep and live life before it all started again. (Talk about your Möbius strips.) Many a day—or night because there is no difference between them for new parents—I fed two children, a bottle in each mouth as the *Twin Peaks* soundtrack played. The twins were consuming the music of Angelo Badalamenti just about as often as they were consuming formula. After a few months of sleeping only a maximum of two consecutive hours, I was, to quote David Bowie, deranged. But I wasn't listening to Bowie sing that song, because I didn't even know *Lost Highway* was a movie, nor that it was released February 21, 1997, almost a month to the day that my twins were released. The twins were not named Alice and Renee, because I had one boy and one girl. By the time the VHS was released in August of that year, I still had not slept more than two consecutive hours, but I was at least sufficiently accustomed to the routine and was back to keeping up with pop culture. So I knew there was a Lynch movie coming out on home video, and I wanted to see it right away.

If you read my *Fire Walk With Me* book, then you know that I was an employee at my local video store when *Fire Walk With Me* was released, and I may, or may not, have stolen a VHS copy the day it came out. But when *Lost Highway* was released four years later, I knew no one who worked at the video store. Four years in retail is like three lifetimes. The place had a complete employee turnover in that amount of time. Plus, I wasn't renting movies anymore. Enjoying life was over for me—I was a parent. Since I had no connections, I was concerned that I might not be able to rent a copy of *Lost Highway* the day it came out. I feared that everyone in town would be trying to get the few copies the store would have for rent. One of the reasons I was so excited to see it was because I had been in such a parenting stupor when the film was released that I didn't know a thing about it. Not one speck. This is how I still like to consume films. If I knew I was going to watch the film, why would I ever watch the preview? They just ruin the movie anyway.

On the morning of August 12, 1997, I packed up the twins and got to the video store when it opened. Again, for my faithful readers, of course I was nervous that they would arrest me for stealing the *Fire Walk With Me* poster, promos, and the thermos, but I held my head high as I balanced my son and daughter and made a beeline for the Drama section of the video store. Hmm, no *Lost Highway*. I waddled to—what? Action/Adventure? Maybe they put it there. Nope. What was going on? They didn't even get the film? Or did the employees not put the videos out on the floor yet? When I worked there, I always had the videotapes out as soon as we opened. Could the entire video rental world have collapsed in four short years?

I went up to the desk and asked, "Where is the new David Lynch movie? Are they all rented out already?" The young punk, who had been me just a presidential term ago, looked at me like I was 107 years old. Had he never seen a man holding two children and two Teletubbies before?

"Settle, dude. They're still there. It's right there in horror."

Horror? David Lynch made a horror film? How long had I been out? I went over to that section and all three copies of *Lost Highway* were still sitting there. I picked up a copy and headed home. Horror? This didn't sound promising. I still woke up in a puddle of sweat thinking about Bob climbing over the Hayward couch. I wasn't feeling great about this. Plus, the two-hour-and-nine-minute run time was just outside the two-hour twin cycle, so it was going to take perfect execution for me to watch the film uninterrupted. I had an hour to feed the twins, put them down, and immediately start the video. I sat on the floor, a child on each side of me and the VHS videotape resting in the plastic container in front of me. Just staring at the tape and dreaming of watching a new David Lynch film was thrilling. When they finished and I placed them in their cribs, I went downstairs and popped the videotape into the machine, and it automatically started to play. I turned the lights out and fast-forwarded through the pointless previews. This was in the phase of my life where I was watching my VHS copy of *Fire Walk With Me* nonstop, so I was superexcited to watch something new by my favorite director.

The credits were a revelation to me. As I mentioned, I didn't follow any of the information when the movie was released, so I had no idea who was in it. Richard Pryor? Marilyn Manson? Robert Blake? Wasn't he Baretta? So interesting. The credits were busy and dark. The yellow lettering coming and going like smashed bugs on a windshield. The film started with a bit of a mystery with the "Dick Laurent is dead" comment, but how did Bill Pullman hear this? Who said it? I couldn't even see what he was talking into. The film was so blurry and dark. I had my volume turned all the way up, which didn't really help with the dialogue—it just caused the hissing sound that all VHS tapes naturally make, even louder. Patricia Arquette came out in all black—was that even her? The film was so dark that even her hair was black. She also looked stretched and as if she was half cut off. The pan-and-scan version of the VHS was blocking us from seeing what Lynch wanted us to see, and the color was horrible. I couldn't even see the living room at all. The sound was unsettling. Then Bill Pullman went to a bar and started playing the saxophone, and it was superloud. No problem hearing that. I plunged the volume down as quickly as I could. The sound of the saxophone was relentless. If you have not seen this part of the movie, I can only describe the sound in one way. It sounded like two newborn babies screaming. It went on and on; the lights were blinking. It was loud. I got up and ejected that videotape and popped it back into its case. I wasn't even kind and I didn't even

You think this capture is dark? On the VHS version, you couldn't tell that was a red dress. Photo courtesy of Peter Deming

rewind. It had hardly played at all. I didn't have time for this. The lights were already out in the basement. I laid back down enjoying the silence and fell asleep and went back to living the same three hours over and over again on repeat for another few months.

In 1999, I saw *The Straight Story* on opening day in the theater. In 2001, I saw *Mulholland Dr.* the day it came out. I loved them both. But I never went back to try *Lost Highway*. All I could think of was that horrible saxophone sound. And the video clerk telling me the film was a horror film. Neither of those things made me want to revisit it. I, like everyone else in America, just forgot about the film. It wasn't until the winter of 2017 when we were prepping Issue #7 of *The Blue Rose* magazine that I realized I had better watch *Lost Highway*. In that issue, we were picking forty female characters to cover for our *Women of Lynch* magazine. I didn't want to admit to Courtenay Stallings, who oversaw the issue, that I had never seen the film. That winter, I watched all of Lynch's films in order. I was really dreading watching *Lost Highway*. I put the DVD in and started the film. This time, I loved it. The film was still dark, but at least I could see that it was Patricia Arquette. She didn't have black hair; it was actually more red. Her lipstick and dress were amazing. To me she looked like Bettie Page. Yes, the saxophone solo was crazy, but it wasn't as much of an aural assault as some of his other work. That summer, I had seen *Twin Peaks: The Return*. I'd sat through "She's Gone" and the atomic explosion in Part 8. This time, Pullman's little solo didn't bother me a bit. Also, there was another factor that made a difference: I was sleeping more than two hours consecutively. The film played completely differently this time, and I loved it so much.

So why take you all the way down this path? Well, for two reasons. First, because the mood that a viewer is in has a ton to do with how they consume a film. It's why I am always willing to give a movie a second chance, especially with a David Lynch film. Therefore, if you were just like me and you loved *Twin Peaks* but haven't given *Lost Highway* a chance because of its horror label, or how you felt about it twenty-five years ago, things have changed. Try again. *Lost Highway* editor Mary Sweeney told me in 2021, "David is avant-garde. He's an avant-garde filmmaker, meaning literally he is leading. He is out in the lead. He's forging a trail. When I show *Lost Highway* in a class I teach at USC, nonlinear things do not bother students now. So the fact that the character changes from Bill Pullman to Balthazar Getty and it becomes a different movie just doesn't faze audiences now. He was just ahead of the curve. It was a brilliant idea. And he was challenged a lot on that plot at the time." Everyone knows that Lynch is considered avant-garde, but then they are surprised when his films are ahead of what everyone else is doing at the time.

Second, I felt it was important to come clean that I am not a lifelong fan of the film. It's OK if it takes a while to understand *Twin Peaks: The Return*, *Mulholland Dr.*, or *Lost Highway*. I'll be totally honest and admit I am still trying to make sense out of *Inland Empire*. But I will someday. (I wouldn't wait on the book, though.) Lynch followed up his film *Fire Walk With Me* with *Lost Highway*. Here I am, following up my book *Fire Walk With Me: Your Laura Disappeared* with *Lost*

Highway: The Fist of Love. But just like the films, this book is not a sequel. *Fire Walk With Me* is a personal film to me, *Lost Highway* isn't. It's something I respect and appreciate, but it is also sort of new to me. For this book, I will leave most of the talking to the cast and crew. The twenty-fifth anniversary of *Lost Highway* was in 2022, and Lynch celebrated by releasing a new 4K print of the film. Because of that, I decided that Issue #17 of *The Blue Rose* would cover *Lost Highway.* I figured I'd do four short pages on it. So I reached out to Patricia Arquette (Renee/Alice) for an interview. I knew she would never say yes, but I thought I'd start there. She graciously and incredibly agreed to do the interview. So did Natasha Gregson Wagner (Sheila). Then Balthazar Getty (Pete) said he would talk to me. Production assistant Sabrina S. Sutherland was happy to talk, and she led me to DP Peter Deming and cameraman Scott Ressler. Producer Deepak Nayar wanted to weigh in on his experiences. You won't be disappointed in his stories, trust me. Deepak had a singular relationship with David Lynch, and he tells such fun stories about their time together. (He shares a great

Issue #17 of *The Blue Rose* inspired the writing of this book.
Cover by Tom Christophersen

Fire Walk With Me story that should have been in my last book, but I printed it in this one because it was too fun to leave out.) Makeup artist Debbie Zoller was the one who created the color differences of the two sides of Patricia Arquette's performances of Renee and Alice. I had interviewed her years ago, and she agreed to talk again. With all that, I knew I had gathered more information than was going to fit on four pages in a magazine. Since I had interviewed so many of the principal players, I felt the best way to cover this film was to just listen to the creative people who had helped David Lynch get his vision out into the world. The main missing players, including Bill Pullman, David Lynch, Barry Gifford, and Angelo Badalamenti, don't like to talk about their work. I also didn't try to get the controversial players from the film because that is just not my style. But I was able to find interview quotes from the past from most of the people who passed on being interviewed for the book.

Since this is the forgotten Lynch film, I explain the plot of the movie with as little interpretation as possible in Chapter Two. This way if you haven't paid attention to *Lost Highway* for a decade or two, this chapter will prepare you for the interviews that follow. In Chapter Three, I go through the shooting script and point out what was cut and highlight differences between the finished film and the written script. Here is also where I begin to explain a bit of my overall theory on how the film is not as complex as it seems upon first viewing. The next few chapters contain interviews with the cast and crew. In the middle of the book, I provide a rest stop to discuss the amazing soundtrack, which was the most successful part of the film. Each track on the soundtrack is discussed—where it plays in the film and a bit of the song's history. The rest of the book returns to the interviews with the cast and crew. These Q&As are focused on the craft and skill of each person. After conducting each interview, I was always amazed at the amount of work that each of these artists put in to create this shared piece of art. Add all this up, put it all together, and you get *The Fist of Love*.

If you don't get the "Fist of Love" reference, that's OK. It's a bit of a deep cut. I absolutely love the opening credits song: David Bowie's "I'm Deranged." I wanted the title for this book to come from Bowie's

"I'm Deranged" is written by David Bowie and Brian Eno and
was originally released on Bowie's 1995 album *Outside*.
Photo courtesy of Arista

lyrics. Lynch himself said in his book *Room to Dream*, "Bowie's song
'I'm Deranged' was perfect for the opening; the lyrics are just right." I
couldn't agree more. I searched the lyrics for something that summed
up the movie. The fist of love certainly describes Fred and his violent
attraction to Renee as well as Mr. Eddy's dangerous obsession with
Alice. These violent men love their women with their fists, not their
heart. Fred Madison is the fist of love. He is the monster of the film.

This is a movie that blends something as beautiful as love with
something as disgusting as murder. *Lost Highway* is a difficult movie
to take in. When David Lynch focuses his attention on a topic, it's
always going to be done with no barriers between the characters and
the safety of the audience. Murder is not fun. It's not entertaining. It's
horrifying. It's dark. It's scary, and in our violent culture, it's committed
over and over at the hands of jealous men who feel they own the bodies
of sexually confident, strong, self-sustaining females. It's why the film
is such a piece of art. It takes something so dark and makes something

emotionally satisfying and beautiful out of it. Walking away from the film with a complete understanding of what David Lynch is trying to show can take more than just a bit of thinking on the part of the viewer. I wasn't up for the task when I was a twenty-seven-year-old stay-at-home father of twin infants. I just wasn't as ready then as I am now. Another way to put it might be that back then, I was a sleep-deprived father who wasn't capable of finding the art in the middle of all that noise, and now—I'M DERANGED.

The two sides of Patricia Arquette in *Lost Highway*. Original art drawn by Wayne Barnes for Issue #7 of *The Blue Rose* magazine.

CHAPTER 2
THE MYSTERY, MAN

"I don't know if anyone could make
heads or tails of this material."
—Gene Siskel, 1997

Well, Mr. Siskel, I see your challenge and accept. I believe that with just a little bit of work, anyone can make heads *and* tails of this material. I would even be so bold as to say that it's not even Lynch's most complex film. It just takes a little bit of thought and a moment of research. But critics didn't have time for that. The nineties were full of brave, wonderful, and grown-up films. I am a big fan of movies from the nineties. It will always be my favorite decade of cinema. There was room for all kinds of successful movies, like *Pulp Fiction, Beauty and the Beast, The Crying Game, Pretty Woman, The Ice Storm, Wayne's World,* and *Bridges of Madison County. Lost Highway* could have slipped in there as well. Every brand of movie had a shot in the nineties.

The film begins with a shot of a dark highway where only the yellow lines of the street are visible. This is an exciting opening-credits sequence scored by the David Bowie song "I'm Deranged." In the next scene, Fred Madison (Bill Pullman) sits on his bed smoking a cigarette in the dark. An automatic curtain slides open allowing the sunlight to pour into his room. Fred hears the intercom system buzz, and walks over to it and listens to the person at the front door. A voice says, "Dick Laurent is dead." Fred doesn't have easy access to see who is at the front door. By the time he makes it to a window, there is nobody there. Within a minute of the opening of the film, we have our first question. Who is Dick Laurent? Who said this to Fred? Why are they telling him? This might be the quickest any Lynch film sets up a mystery.

Fred prepares to go to work. He is a saxophone player in a nightclub. His wife, Renee Madison (Patricia Arquette), decides she isn't going to watch him play. She wants to stay home and read a book. This idea seems crazy to Fred. Renee is a brunette who wears a stunning dress and looks like she is well-off. She has the look of the fifties movie star Bettie Page.

Fred goes to the club and plays a crazy saxophone solo that the crowd loves as the lights strobe to the crazy beat. After his solo, he calls his wife at home; the phone rings, but no one answers. When Fred arrives at home, Renee is peacefully sleeping. The next morning, Renee wakes up, and goes outside to get the morning paper. There is a blank manila envelope on the steps with an unmarked videotape inside. Fred and Renee pop it into the VCR and watch a short video of the outside of their house. After a few seconds, it cuts to static.

That night, Fred lies in bed waiting for Renee and remembers playing the crazy saxophone solo. This time, he sees Renee leave the club with a man with a pencil mustache. Was Renee there with another man? Renee gets in bed, and Fred initiates a sexual encounter with her. The sex is lackluster, and Fred struggles to climax. It appears he doesn't because Renee, in a very condescending way, pats him on his back and says, "It's OK." Fred has a look of shame mixed with anger as he rolls over and turns his back to her. He mentions a dream he had where he saw her in bed, but it wasn't her. As he tells Renee the dream, she sits up and her face is no longer her own; it is the face of a Mystery Man (Robert Blake). He jumps back and Renee's face returns.

The next morning, another tape arrives. This video has the same beginning, but the tape runs a little longer. This time, it shows Renee and Fred sleeping in their bed. The position of the camera is high above their bed, and the scene couldn't have been filmed by hand. They call the police, and two detectives are sent out to investigate. They ask if Fred and Renee sleep in the same bed (they do), if they have an alarm system (they do but didn't activate it), and if they own a video camera (they don't because Fred doesn't like them). Fred says he likes to remember things his own way, not exactly as they occurred. The detectives search the perimeter of the house. Fred stays inside but can hear them on the roof. He looks up through a sky light and sees the detective staring down at him.

That night, Renee and Fred go to a party at Andy's house. Andy is the guy with the pencil mustache whom Fred remembered seeing Renee leave the club with. Andy and Renee laugh as they talk, and Fred doesn't like it. Renee asks Fred to get her another drink. As he does, the man whose face Fred saw overlaid on Renee's the night before approaches him. The Mystery Man is pale white, with a very strange demeanor. He tells Fred that he, the Mystery Man, has met Fred before at Fred's house and is actually at his house right now. He invites Fred to call his own home, and when Fred calls from a cell phone, sure enough, the Mystery Man answers the phone. He laughs

Fred and Renee call the police to find out how someone is filming them in their house. Photo courtesy of Peter Deming

and walks off. Fred asks Andy who that man is, and he says that the Mystery Man is a friend of Dick Laurent's. Fred immediately says that Dick Laurent is dead. This upsets Andy, and Renee gets curious as to what they are discussing and who is dead. Fred has no time for answering questions, and they leave the party.

On the ride home, Renee says that she knows Andy because he once got her a job when she needed one but can't remember what job it was. Fred searches the house when they arrive home, but no one is there. As they get ready for bed, Fred looks around the house one more time. He stares down their dark hallway and walks into the darkness. Renee comes out of the bathroom and calls for Fred, but she doesn't see him. The next morning, another tape appears; Fred watches it alone. The tape shows Fred on the floor covered in blood beside Renee's mutilated body. There is a jump cut to Fred getting punched in the face by one of the detectives. Fred is in custody with the police. He is now accused of murdering Renee. Fred proclaims that he didn't kill her but then asks the cops to tell him that he didn't kill her.

Fred is found guilty and sentenced to death by the electric chair and is placed on death row. In the cell, he starts to get bad headaches and begs the guards to help him. After a few days, the guards look in the cell, but Fred isn't there. Pete Dayton (Balthazar Getty) is there. Pete has a huge welt on his forehead but has no idea how he got in the prison or where Fred went. With no reason to hold Pete, the guards call his parents (Gary Busey and Lucy Butler) to take him home. Pete doesn't say much, and his friends come to pick him up to take him out where he dances with his girlfriend Sheila (Natasha Gregson Wagner). She asks him what happened to him, but they dance instead. Unbeknownst to him, Pete is followed everywhere he goes by the police.

Pete goes back to work at Arnie's garage, where his boss (Richard Pryor) is very glad to see him. Mr. Eddy (Robert Loggia) is one of Pete's best clients, and Mr. Eddy doesn't like the sound of his car. He takes Pete for a drive to fix it, which Pete does easily. While they are test-driving the car, a man tailgates Mr. Eddy. He doesn't react well to this. In fact, he lets the stooge pass him, rams him from behind, pulls

Pete tends to Mr. Eddy's vehicular needs.
Photo courtesy of Ciby 2000

him out of the car and beats him with his gun while he tells him the rules of the road. Mr. Eddy pulls himself back together and drives Pete back to the garage, offers him a porno tape (I guess as a tip???), which Pete declines.

The next day, Pete works on a car with a coworker (Jack Nance), and the music on the radio is Fred Madison's crazy saxophone solo from the club. This gives Pete a headache, and he changes the channel. Mr. Eddy pulls up in a different car, and this time he is accompanied by the most beautiful blonde in the world, Alice Wyatt (played again by Patricia Arquette). Pete and Alice share a special glance and later that day Alice returns to the garage alone to ask Pete out. He pointlessly tries to decline, but no one is going to say no to someone in the dress that Alice is wearing. They have sex, and before you know it, they are in love.

When Pete gets home, his parents talk to him about the night he disappeared. They explain that there was a man with him, but they don't tell him more than that. The next time he meets with Alice, she worries that Mr. Eddy knows that they are having an affair. She comes up with a plan that if they rob Andy (the same Andy from the party that Fred and Renee went to), they could escape from Mr. Eddy and run away. Pete asks how she got mixed up with these people. She repeats Renee's dialogue and says that Andy got her a job when she needed it. The film cuts to a scene from the past in which Alice walks into a room of men with Mr. Eddy sitting in the center. A man holds a gun to Alice's head, and without words, Mr. Eddy implies she is there to service him. Alice strips and gets on her knees in between his legs. Pete hates this memory and gets jealous. They make a plan to rob Andy.

Pete arrives at Andy's house, per the plan, and a porno is projected on the wall of Andy's living room. The porno stars in the film are Alice and two other actors (metal rock star Marilyn Manson and Twiggy Ramirez). Andy comes downstairs, Pete hits him on the head, and then accidentally kills him in a fight. Pete sees a picture of Mr. Eddy, Alice, Renee, and Andy. Alice doesn't acknowledge Renee but does point herself out in the picture. Pete's nose starts bleeding, and he goes upstairs to clean up. Upstairs now looks like a hotel, with numbers on the door. He opens a door, and inside the room is another version of Renee/Alice, this one with red hair, who is having sex with Mr. Eddy.

Alice drives Pete to a cabin in the desert. No one is there; Alice and Pete have sex on the sand, basking in the glow from the headlights of

Lost Highway Hotel is the scene of the crime for Fred.
Photo courtesy of Janus Films

the car. Pete says over and over how he wants Alice. She whispers in his ear, "You'll never have me." She gets up and walks to the cabin. When Pete stands up, he is Fred (Bill Pullman). He goes into the cabin, and the Mystery Man is there; Alice is gone. The Mystery Man says that her name isn't Alice, it's Renee.

Fred gets out of there and stops at a place called the Lost Highway Hotel. While Fred is walking down the hotel hallway, it becomes clear this is the same hallway that Pete walked down in the upstairs of Andy's house. This time it is Fred who opens the hotel door to see the character we know as Mr. Eddy in Pete's story, who is now called Dick Laurent in Fred's version, having sex with Renee. Fred waits until Renee leaves, and then he grabs Laurent, puts him in the trunk of his car, and drives out to the desert. Fred wants to make it clear to Laurent that the reason he is about to kill him is because of Laurent's relationship with Renee. So the Mystery Man and Fred show Laurent the porno of Renee on a portable TV screen. The Mystery Man shoots Laurent, but after he dies, the Mystery Man is gone and Fred is the one holding the gun. Fred heads back to the Madison house and speaks into the front door intercom, "Dick Laurent is dead." The police show up, and Fred jumps in the same car that Mr. Eddy drove when he chased the tailgater. The police chase Fred down the highway from the opening credits. They keep getting closer, and Fred starts to convulse, and his face starts distorting. The film ends.

***

Before moving on, I have to admit it was kind of fun to write out the plot of *Lost Highway*. I have been studying the film quite a bit over the last month for all the interviews that are contained in the book, and I even just saw the 4K restoration a few days ago. I did double-check a few things but most of that is just right from my brain, which I think means I truly am deranged. In some ways, I can see how the film is confusing for a first-time viewer. Even more so to a viewer who has never seen a David Lynch film before. Almost every single film ever made explains everything that happens. *Lost Highway* just doesn't spoon-feed the answers to you. I will explain more specific connections as the book goes on, but just from the simplest explanation, the film is

Fred's fantasy of what happened. He admits in the movie that he likes to remember things his way, not exactly as they actually happened. I mean, that is pretty clear. Not sure why Gene Siskel couldn't crack that code. Also, the other simple thing to keep in mind is that Pete is totally a projection of Fred's mind. There is no Pete, no Sheila, no Alice.

In the end, all the confusion that critics and filmgoers had back in 1997 was really just the mystery, man. It is just an old-fashioned noir film that leaves you wondering, nervous, unsettled, and with the fun of figuring out how everything connects. Going back to where we began with O. J. Simpson, this film was Lynch wondering how a murderer could convince himself that he was innocent. If you keep that in your mind, along with these simple facts:

- Fred is not a reliable narrator
- Pete and Alice aren't real
- Fred never escaped from jail

Then, I believe, you can make heads and tails out of the film. I believe this book, along with the help of the many creative people who made the film, will explain the film and help any viewer understand what Lynch was trying to achieve with this piece of art. Aren't you excited? Soon you'll be remembering the film the way you want and not the way Fred wanted.

CHAPTER 3
"STAY HOME. READ."

A 21st Century Noir Horror Film.
A graphic investigation into parallel identity crises.
A world where time is dangerously out of control.
A terrifying ride down the lost highway.
—David Lynch 21 June 1995

The lines printed above are what begins the David Lynch-Barry Gifford original script. This was the third time the two had cowritten a screenplay. They had worked together on 1990's *Wild at Heart* and 1993's *Hotel Room* for HBO. Barry Gifford said in *Pretty as a Picture: The Art of David Lynch*, "David called up and said, 'BARRY, we've *got* to write a movie.' So I said, 'OK, but I am working on this new novel now, and I can't really do it right now.' And he said, 'No, Barry, we have to write a new movie, and we have to do it now.' So I said, 'Well, I'm not going anywhere.' He said, 'Stay right there. I'm coming up.'" David Lynch said on the DVD bonus features, "Barry and I were talking about writing something together, and I guess one day I had some ideas, and he had some ideas, and I flew up to Berkeley, and we sat down in his office, and I told him my ideas, and then he told me his ideas, and we both hated each other's ideas. So we sat there for a little bit and then I said, 'Well, I have a little idea.' And he said, 'Well, I kind of like that,' and one thing led to another and there was *Lost Highway.*'"

Gifford and Lynch wrote the script during the summer of 1995, two years after their last project together. In this chapter, I will point out notable differences between the script and the finished film. I don't know if these changes were filmed and edited out or cut before they were ever filmed. Lynch famously gets ideas while he is directing, so some changes might have caused certain lines or scenes to be different. A prime example of that is the exploding cabin, which appears throughout the film but was not in the script anywhere. You will discover why that is when you read the interviews later in the book. For now, I will walk you through the script and provide a few insights into how I interpret the film, and why things were cut to sharpen the story that Lynch wanted to tell.

The beginning of the script describes the darkened street-level shot of the yellow lines on a highway that opens the film. The written text for the first scene describes how Fred is looking at himself in the mirror as he smokes. The shot that we see in the film could be a mirror reflection, but since Lynch never cuts to a long shot or an establishing shot, there is no way of knowing if what we see is actually

Is this opening shot a reflection in a mirror? The script says yes.
Photo courtesy of Ciby 2000/Criterion

a reflection in the mirror or just Fred smoking on the bed. It certainly doesn't matter for any plot purposes, but it would be interesting to know what is in the film just because the pilot of *Twin Peaks* begins with Josie Packard (Joan Chen) looking in a mirror. So it would be somewhat of interest to know if both projects start the same way. But really, only of interest for Lynch obsessives like myself.

The script describes Fred sitting in the dark on the bed and then a mechanical curtain opens, letting the sunlight into the room. I think the sound, as well as the lights sliding across his face, suggests that a prison door is being slid open. To me, Fred is already in prison. I don't mean figuratively. I mean in reality. He is having this fantasy while he is in jail, on death row.

The film's "Dick Laurent is dead" scene appears exactly as scripted. So where did Lynch get this idea from? According to him, this actually happened. Lynch said in the bonus features, "The whole thing in the beginning happened to me. The intercom buzzer went off early one morning and a voice said, 'David.' And I said, 'Yes?' And the voice said, 'Dick Laurent is dead.' Now I didn't have a window to look at right then. So I went from where I was to a different part of the house so I could try to see if anybody was leaving the house who had said that. And I saw no one. By the time I went to the window where I could see out, there was no one there." While David Lynch just filed this strange moment away and went on with his life, Dick Laurent is not going to just become a passing thought for Fred Madison.

In the script, after the Madisons watch the first video, Renee eats breakfast and reads her book. Fred asks her if this book is the same one she was reading the night she didn't go to the club. She says it isn't and reminds him that he could have woken her up when he got home. The point of this scene is to show Fred's jealousy, but since it's really only the third scene, I am not sure we need this *and* the scene where he imagines Renee going off with Andy. This was a good cut. However, as a publisher, I like that Renee is reading books this quickly. Maybe she could buy one or two of mine?

In the script's version of the sex scene between Fred and Renee, Fred does climax, and Renee pats his back "consolingly." I never viewed this scene that way. I always felt this scene plays out like he couldn't climax, or maybe couldn't even perform, and that is why she sympathetically pats him on the back. I guess either way, Renee does not climax and isn't satisfied by the sex with Fred, and that is the point.

In the following scene, Fred tells Renee about a dream he had in which he searched for her and then found her in bed. During his voice-over, his line is typed as: "It <u>looked</u> like you . . . but it wasn't," the word looked is underlined. Obviously, no one watching the film knows that the word is underlined in the script, but this certainly is a clue that Alice, who looks like Renee, isn't Renee. The line of dialogue certainly sets up viewers for the fact that when you get to his extended dream part of the movie, Patricia Arquette isn't playing the same character. Not that any viewer could know that on first viewing.

The next morning, Renee finds the second tape. The dog's barking in that scene is included in the script. Renee mentions that the dog woke her, and Fred wonders who owns that dog. To me, this is the barking of a police dog that Fred hears while he is in jail. The dog does not belong in the posh Hollywood neighborhood that they live in, but more of the breed of dog that would work in a prison. Does Fred hear the barking dog in prison?

On the second videotape, it is hard to see who is actually in bed in the film. One could wonder if Fred is actually on the tape. Or does the tape show Renee in bed with someone else? No. According to the script, it is Fred and Renee in bed together. So if Fred is the killer, how could he film this while being in bed with her? Because there never were any tapes delivered to the house with Fred and Renee in bed. This is all fantasy that Fred creates in his own mind to let him off the hook for murdering his wife. In the fantasy, it is the Mystery Man who recorded those tapes, which, in a dream-logic way, is true. Fred is the Mystery Man, so he did record these tapes, but all of this is in his mind.

Once the detectives arrive, the script and film diverge again. The script has them comment on the height of the camera angle and the smoothness of its motion—none of which made it to the film. They comment how the camera is not handheld. I'm not overly surprised that this was cut. I don't think that Lynch would have liked that this scene pointed out something that the viewer should notice for themselves. He likes when viewers come up with theories and discuss them afterward. I think the way the cameras are positioned on the videotapes are very much how security footage looks, again pointing us back to the fact that Fred is actually a prisoner in jail where he is being watched all the time.

The script spells out most of the camera shots. Lynch, as shown in the *Twin Peaks: The Return* bonus features, sees the movie in his head before he shoots it. One shot that was not mentioned is the skylight of the detective looking down at Fred. Most likely in writing the script, Lynch didn't know the house they would shoot in would have a skylight. This shot corroborates the "Fred's actually in jail the entire time" theory, as the composition of the shot is repeated when Fred is actually shown in jail looking at the light overhead. [See images below]

In the top two shots, Fred is at home; in the bottom shots, he is in jail. But is this actually the same moment—one real and the other unfolding only in his imagination?
Photo courtesy of Ciby 2000

In my reading of the film, and producer Deepak Nayar will back me up on this in a later chapter, very little of what viewers see in the movie actually happened. The two parts of the film that truly happened are the police chase in which Fred tries to escape, and the brief scene where the detectives investigate Andy's murder and see the photo of Mr. Eddy, Renee, and Andy. Everything else is the way that Fred likes to remember it. "Not necessarily the way they happened." So did a videotape arrive at their doorstep? I say no. But if it did, it was Fred torturing Renee into thinking that someone was watching them so that he could scare her out of having her affairs with Dick Laurent and Andy. But I don't believe she was *ever* unfaithful to Fred. I think the infidelity was all in his head. It doesn't really matter if the videotapes arrived or didn't. They are setting the stage for the fact that Renee lives in a house of fear. Fred might have sent her videotapes so she would think someone was watching her, and then she would have to stop the affairs that Fred believed she committed. Maybe he made up that they were getting the tapes only in his fantasy because it was easier for him to believe that she lived in fear because of them and not because of him. There are plenty of options. You can pick the one that you like best.

The fact that the tapes are filmed from a vantage point that no one could ever film them from lends credence to my understanding that the tapes do not really exist. But since this is Fred's fantasy that we are witnessing, maybe in his memory that is what the tapes looked like. For all we know, they weren't shot this expertly with smoothness and perfection. Maybe his finger was over the lens and at one point he caught his own reflection in one of the mirrors, Renee saw it was him and said, "Fred, what the heck? That's you in the mirror. What are you trying to pull here?" Then he had to kill her. In the film, she does say that Fred doesn't like video cameras, and maybe that is why. I like this comedic theory and enjoy pretending this would have been entitled: *Lost Highway: The On the Air* edition. Nonsense aside, my point is that when you are reading any part of the film, you always have to remember that it is filtered through a madman. (That is also good advice for reading this book.)

The next scene after the detectives arrive in the film is the party at

Renee leaves with another man (Andy), but did this happen?
Photo courtesy of Ciby 2000/Criterion

Andy's house, where we meet the Mystery Man. In the script, there is a cut scene where Fred is on stage playing another sax solo, and he sees Renee leave the club with two unidentified men. In the film, this happens before their lackluster sexual encounter, and we also see that she is with Andy, even though in the film we don't know who Andy is until the party scene.

In the script, he sees Renee leave with two unidentified men. One can only speculate that it would have been Andy and Mr. Eddy. In the film, she definitely leaves with only one man, Andy. Following the scene at the club, the Madisons receive a third videotape. This tape begins the same way. Exterior of the house. Then the hallway. Then the couple in bed. The new footage on the third tape is Fred waking and sitting up in bed stretching his head up to look directly into the camera, then a quick cut to static. As they react to this new footage, Renee screams and says there was something else on the tape. Fred rewinds and pauses on a quick half-second clip of Fred on his knees on the floor of Renee's side of the bed with a grimace on his face, his eyes wide with terror.

The detectives return and ask if they have any enemies. They don't. They ask if they used the alarm system, and Fred says only the first night, but he hasn't since because he doesn't like to be paranoid. Renee hadn't known this information. She is not pleased and wants to stay at a hotel.

After these three scenes, the script and film sync up again, and Andy's party is next. The script does say that the party is hosted by one of the men whom Fred saw Renee leaving with at his nightclub, which is interesting because the script said there were two men, both unidentified. The script says this is the man she left with, so it was like Gifford and Lynch decided that Renee would just leave the bar with Andy and forgot to go back earlier in the script and change the two men to just Andy. Also, the scene where she leaves with Andy didn't seem to be a recollection from Fred in the script. In the film, it is intercut with Fred in bed thinking about it as we see Renee leave with Andy. The script made it seem like it was an actual scene where Renee truly left with Andy. The film makes us wonder, was she home that night? Or out with Andy?

Andy's party and their drive home is written basically the same as the film. The only difference is a short line in the script about déjà vu by Renee after Fred checks their house when they get home. Also, the script doesn't say that Fred sees a flash of light in their house when he arrives home. Renee says she has a feeling Fred told her to wait outside while he checked the house before.

The next change from script to screen is after Renee is dead and Fred is punched by the detective. Renee's body is in the morgue. The medical examiner arrives in a tuxedo with a young, slinky girl named Joyce on his arm. She is nervous, and he just came from a party at the mayor's house. Renee's body is all packaged up like meat from a butcher's shop with labels on each body part. In one interestingly staged shot, the camera follows a burning cigarette tossed to the floor by the medical examiner. The ME and his girlfriend can be heard talking, but the cigarette is all we see until Joyce's high heels walk into the shot as Joyce, disgusted by the unwrapping of Renee's body parts, leaves the room. Cutting this scene was a wise decision, since it's unlikely Fred would have envisioned any of this, but I would love to have seen how Lynch would have filmed this scene. I bet it would have been beautiful.

The following scene is the reading of the verdict. We do hear the judge sentence Fred in the film, but in the script we see the jury, the courtroom, and the reading of the verdict. Fred faints at the guilty verdict and then looks up as if he is being filmed from a video camera that is up high, continuing the surveillance feeling that the film has through the first act.

Following his sentencing is a scene in a lingerie shop where two of Andy's girls search for lingerie and discuss the case of the husband who chopped his wife into a million pieces. They also discuss the different ways of being executed and which they would choose. Andy sneaks up behind one of them and surprises them.

This is followed by an execution sequence of an inmate named Sammy G. The other inmates wish him well and tell him to be brave. Fred says nothing, but he shakes as Sammy is taken through all the steps of electrocution. When he is finally electrocuted, the camera is on Fred in his cell, where the light above him dims and then the electricity goes out. It's hard to say whether having this in the film would have been beneficial or not. On the positive side, it would have made the film slightly political to actually show an execution, as well as the discussion between the two girls about the ways the state kills people. It also connects to a theory that many people have that this entire fantasy is what goes through Fred's mind as he is electrocuted. The first person I ever heard put forth this theory was Mya McBriar in Issue #7 of *The Blue Rose*. So showing an electrocution in the film would have connected nicely. The negative side is that it would have slowed down the film. Also, I like that the only two connections in the film to electrocution are the voice over from the judge saying Fred is sentenced to death by electrocution and the final scene of the film, when he is driving and his face seems to burn off.

Before Fred transforms into Pete, there are two scenes that are described in the script that aren't in the film. The Madison house is shown from outside, and it has a for sale sign in front of it and is filmed in the same way that the videotape was shot. This makes Renee's claim of the tapes being from a real estate agent something first time viewers can cling to. Then, the two girls from the lingerie store are shown wearing what they purchased and dancing around Andy who is laying on the floor and too drugged up to move. They dance and party.

The script describes a more literal transformation of Fred. He vomits and bleeds from the nose and then rolls around in his mess. Then his face loses all features and is just a white mass with eye sockets. The script describes the same scene of the headlights on the highway turning towards Pete, but then the camera goes back to the cell where the white mass pieces together the features of Pete and we actually see Fred become Pete. My guess is this was too expensive to film. It could be done pretty easily in 2023 with special effects, but in 1996, I am sure they didn't have the budget to do something like that. Also, it's a better reveal to have the prison guard find him the next morning and for us to not know what creeps out the guard when he looks in the cell. Money and special effects don't always make a movie better. Sorry Disney.

There are two scenes that were cut that have the police trying to figure out where Fred went. They take blood from Pete and try to question him, but he can't seem to talk. The actions in these scenes are covered in the movie when the prison staff talks about who Pete is. So these are good cuts.

The warden talks about the press getting wind of Fred's escape, and the guards search the prison cell to see if there was a way for Fred to escape. The guard even looks in the toilet to see if Fred could flush himself out of the cell. The warden also talks to the press saying that Fred escaped but doesn't mention that Pete appeared. The warden and the doctor then question Pete's parents, who have no information to share. They bring Pete in and ask him routine questions, none of which he can answer. He can speak, but it is slow and strained. The police want to hold him, but they have no legal reason to, so they let him go. After the parents and Pete leave, the warden instructs the guards to have Pete followed.

These are all normal procedural scenes that normal movies have. Removing them makes the movie feel stranger because the film doesn't follow the Hollywood formula of how a summer blockbuster movie would handle a plot point where one guy turns into another guy. We don't want to sit through the normal beats of a Hollywood script when we are watching a David Lynch movie. Removing these classic police-procedural scenes probably earned the film all those bad reviews, but

This publicity photo captures a scene that was not in the final cut.
Photo courtesy of Ciby 2000

it earns props with true Lynch fans. The other way to look at it, is that these cuts make it so much more of Fred's fantasy. These cut scenes are all pointless to Fred's obsession with Renee and his desire to own her. In his world, the police are not heroes; they are feckless.

There are two scenes cut with Pete at home with his parents taking care of him. Again, they are normal scenes that could be in any movie. The one line of interest is that just like Fred did in prison, Pete asks for an aspirin for a headache. The script names the two detectives who follow Pete as Ed and Al; these are also the names of the detectives who investigated the videotapes in the first part of the movie. The detectives are played by different actors, but with the same names. In the film, the detectives who follow Pete are named Lou and Hank, not Ed and Al. It would have been cooler if the detectives had the same names.

Pete eats a sandwich and his parents ask him if he remembers anything; he doesn't. They also mention that Arnie is missing him at the garage, and they can't go on without him down there. This is another pointless scene, and we understand all of that when Pete returns to the garage. Good cut.

The scene where the friends come to get Pete to go out to the

A few deleted scenes were filmed at this coffee shop.
Photo courtesy of Fine Cut Presentations

bowling alley, has a bit of cut dialogue where the female friend, Lanie, mentions that they found a cyst on her ovary. So she had it cut out. She pulls her pants down to show a three-inch scar. I have no idea what this symbolizes, but I am glad I don't have to come up with one. There is a scene of them driving to the bowling alley where Pete is disgusted with the sound V's car makes. The character of V is played by Giovanni Ribisi. His name is described as being short for Steven. On the way there, V pulls into a drive-in diner where a group of girls are dancing together in the parking lot. Sheila and the girls come over to the car and Pete invites them to come with them to the bowling alley. One of the girls asks what happened to his face, but Pete doesn't explain anything. The alley plays mostly the same with a few extra lines where Pete asks what happened the last time Sheila saw him, and she won't answer.

The film matches the script until there's a few differences in the tailgating sequence after Mr. Eddy beats up the guy and returns to the car. He asks Pete if he knows how many car lengths it takes to stop at 45 mph, then at 60 mph. Pete knows exactly, and this satisfies Mr. Eddy. Remember that the entire Pete section of the film is what Fred *wishes* his life had been. So of course Pete knows these calculations of how many car lengths it takes to stop. He knows how to fix Mr. Eddy's car as well, and everyone is waiting for him to arrive at the garage because he is a fix-it-yourself man. He is not like Fred at all. He is a young, smart, blue-collar worker.

As for the tailgating scene, why is it in his fantasy at all? What is Fred doing at the end of the movie? He is trying to escape the police. They are getting closer and closer. One could even say the police are *tailgating* him. Of course Mr. Eddy, who is the big bad in Fred's fantasy, hates tailgating. Of course he demoralizes the man who is chasing him. Mr. Eddy even cites the law and demands that the tailgater follow the rules. The police don't set the laws of the world; Fred does. Fred's ultimate fantasy is outsmarting the police. Where are the police when this tailgating sequence happens? They are still sitting outside the garage. They didn't see Pete leave with Mr. Eddy. This was Pete getting "away" from the police, which is what Fred wishes most would happen. The police even see Pete return so that they know that Pete, and therefore Fred, outsmarted them. It isn't enough for Fred to just get away with it; he wants them to know he got away with it. He will be the smartest person. He will best Mr. Eddy, Andy, Alice, Renee, and everyone in the world. Fred is a narcissist and a misogynist who has to be in control of everything. In his fantasy, the police and tailgating are bad; in reality, the police caught Fred and he was sentenced to death.

There is a cut scene of the detectives watching Pete when he is at his house and one of the cops pees in a bottle and then dumps the urine in the street. I bet you're sorry you didn't get to see that scene.

After Alice and Pete meet and have sex, there is a scene of them driving home and Alice suspects that someone is following them. It's the detectives who are following them. Pete loses them at a stoplight. Hmm, another time where Pete outsmarts the police, what could this mean?

The next night, after Alice says she can't see Pete that night because she has to see Mr. Eddy, Pete goes back to the drive-in restaurant. When he shows up, all his friends from the bowling alley are there, including Sheila, who hangs with her girlfriends. While Pete is looking at Sheila, he starts to get upset because she doesn't really notice him. The camera then becomes Sheila's point of view, and Pete is no longer standing with his friends. She literally can't see him. Sheila starts dancing with one of her girlfriends. (This is a scene that is shown in the documentary *Pretty as a Picture*. Deepak Nayar will tell a great story about filming this night in his chapter.) When the camera turns back to Pete's point of view, he can't see, and he starts to get a headache. V asks if he is OK. It is unclear if she also disappeared from his sight or if she just moved away. While this is going on, a drunk guy starts dancing with Sheila. Pete thinks maybe he can't see her because she is on the other side of the building, so he heads that way. When he sees her dancing with the guy, he immediately punches the guy in the nose, and a brawl breaks out. Sheila is surprised that he was there because she couldn't see him. She is impressed that he cares this much. They go to a hotel and have sex. This sex scene is in the movie and the drive-in fight scene would have happened right before this sex scene. Their sex resembles the sex that Fred and Renee had at the beginning of the film, in that Pete has the same vacant stare after the sex ends.

There is a cut phone call between Sheila and Pete after his parents talk to him where Pete tries to get Sheila to tell him about the night that he disappeared and who the man was with him. The scene is written like it would be filmed as a one-sided phone call of Pete talking.

For the sequence where Alice strips for Mr. Eddy at gunpoint, this was written with a voice-over from Alice describing what we see and her talking about her nerves. It was just a few lines and didn't last once she entered the room.

The end of the scene where Alice relays this story to Pete was written with a little more dialogue. In the film, it ends once she makes the plan, but in the script, they start to have sex that turns wild with Alice getting on top and demanding that he says that he is her man. This connects with Fred's desire for Alice to need him and also that she is the one manipulating him to kill Andy. In reality, Fred murdered Renee, Andy, and Dick Laurent, but in the Pete story, he *has* to kill Andy to save Alice from Mr. Eddy (who is Dick Laurent). Fred also believed he had to kill Andy to save Renee from her own desires. We actually don't know if Renee was unfaithful to Fred or not. It is really dealer's choice. In my opinion, Renee never cheated on Fred. She feared him and wasn't into all the sexcapades that Fred believed she was. But I don't have anything to back that up beyond my feeling that Fred was just a true monster.

When Pete gets home after having sex with Alice, Sheila is waiting for him on the front porch. In the script, the first thing she does when she sees Pete is to scream in horror, "There's someone with him." When the camera cuts back to Pete and then back to Sheila, she is no longer afraid and then she delivers her line that is in the film about him being with another girl. Whether this would have been the Mystery Man or Fred doesn't really matter, since they are the same person anyway. Sheila's line would certainly have been a flash from the night that Pete disappeared, since his parents said someone was with him. After Sheila breaks up with him and leaves, Mr. Eddy calls and there is a cut line when the Mystery Man talks to Pete on the phone. The Mystery Man says, "We just killed a couple of people. We thought we'd come over and tell you about it." Mr. Eddy laughs in the background and then goes into the speech about the Far East that is in the movie.

Later when Alice and Pete have killed Andy and are ransacking his house, the picture that shows Renee and Alice along with Mr. Eddy and Andy is in the script and it does describe that when Pete sees it his nose starts to bleed. I believe this happens because this is when the police punch Fred in the nose. They show him the picture of Mr. Eddy, Renee, and Andy. (No Alice in the picture because there is no Alice.) The police got this photograph from Andy's house.

After they rob Andy, in the script they stop at a house where Alice rings the bell, and a houseboy tells them to head to the cabin in the desert. Another good cut; we are ready to get to the cabin. The cabin is in the script, but there's no mention of it exploding or catching fire.

The script plays out the same with Fred reappearing and then escaping to the Lost Highway Hotel. One thing that is of interest is that the script now describes the Robert Loggia character as Mr. Eddy/Laurent. This is because there is no Mr. Eddy. When Fred wakes and right before he kills Laurent, the script describes his movements as the same as in the videotaped sequence of Fred waking up in bed that was cut from the film.

The script and the movie have Renee (not Alice) and Laurent having sex at this hotel. Renee sneaks out of the hotel; Fred enters and attacks Laurent, eventually killing him. So if we see her sneaking away from Laurent, then why in my theory do I think that Renee never had sex with Dick Laurent? Why don't I believe that Renee had sex with Laurent and Andy and that Fred caught her and then killed all three of them? Simple. Because that makes the story less compelling. If Renee cheated on him, then Fred is "justified" in his own mind in murdering all three of them. But it is more likely that as a violent, jealous white man, he feels it is his God-given right to treat her this way due to her supposed infidelity. I submit he was a violent, horrible husband from the get-go that she was afraid of him, and was not a whore before they met, or after. She was nothing more than a victim who was murdered by the hands of a jealous man. Remember that he didn't even believe that she would stay home and read. He had to make it that she was banging some young dude. I think all his paranoia, which starts to infect his Pete avatar the longer the fantasy goes on as well, is just another example of our patriarchal society. I mean, even Tay Tay sings, "Fuck the patriarchy."

When the Mystery Man hands the pocket TV to Mr. Eddy and he watches the porno with Renee in it, the script says, the other two women in the porno are the same two women who were buying lingerie and dancing around Andy in the two cut scenes. These two characters became Marilyn Manson and Twiggy Ramirez, which is probably why all the scenes with them were cut. The rest of the film plays out as scripted. I am not surprised that there aren't any cuts toward the end of the film. One of the things that impresses me most about *Lost Highway* is how strong the ending is. Think of it: this is a David Lynch film that ends with a car chase. Who would have thunk it?

***

The script had a decent amount of scenes that were cut, but everything that was cut makes sense. The majority of the cuts involved procedures from the police that treated the switching of Fred to Pete as something that could be solved or understood. It almost would have turned the film into an episode of *The X-Files* where law enforcement tries to make sense out of a supernatural event. That isn't what this film is, and it was right to cut them out. One could make an argument that keeping the other prisoner's execution would have been important to the film. If Fred is actually having this fantasy while he is being electrocuted, then seeing the other prisoner go through this traumatic experience would be another way of Fred splitting himself off from his reality and instead experiencing the execution as if he was someone else—in the same way he has Pete fall in love with Alice and murder Andy. But my guess is Lynch didn't want to lean too heavily on showing viewers that Fred was electrocuted. He makes that point in more of a Lynchian way by having Fred's face distort and burn in the final scene. In reality, we are shown everything that happens to Fred, just out of order, filtered through Fred's mind, and in a Lynchian way.

The other major cut was the third videotape arriving which showed Fred waking up and looking at the camera. This was followed by Renee and the police reacting to the tape. But did we really need to see them getting four total videotapes? I think the point was made, and it doesn't really add anything, since Fred does get the final tape showing him on tape around her mutilated body. Lynch and editor Mary Sweeney kept the pace of the story and cut all the things that would have slowed the plot down. This pacing is very much in line with the Sweeney years of being Lynch's editor. No one would ever accuse Lynch of having quick pacing, but I think she kept him more in line than other editors. While for many Lynch films fans clamor for the missing pieces, I think it makes sense that the fragments that were cut, remain cut. After all, it was just a terrifying ride down the lost highway.

CHAPTER 4
PATRICIA ARQUETTE

Oh, how male critics love to clutch their pearls and moan and worry about female actresses who act in a David Lynch film. From Isabella Rossellini in *Blue Velvet* to Naomi Watts in *Mulholland Dr.* to Sheryl Lee in *Fire Walk With Me*, there has always been someone to say the actress was put through too much in the film. What would these women do without men to worry about whether they were strong enough to handle a complex role? Isn't it strange that no one ever worried about what Scorsese put De Niro, DiCaprio, or Day-Lewis through? A female role in a Lynch film means the actress is going to have emotionally challenging work to do. She is given more to do than just be eye candy on the arm of a male who gets all the great scenes. Rossellini brings anger and passion to her scenes as a mother who is being tortured by an obsessed fan. Lee brought to life what it is actually like to be abused by a parent. Watts played two versions of how a Hollywood dream can turn out and goes through just about every emotion during the film. Her handling of these scenes put her in the top tier of actresses and made her a superstar in Hollywood. We know which side of the dream her story turned out to be. These examples don't even include all the wonderful scenes that Lynch gave Laura Dern for well over thirty years.

But when film historians are listing great female performances in

Lynch films, rarely does anyone add what Patricia Arquette achieved in *Lost Highway*. (Another piece of evidence to support my lost film theory.) Arquette is cast as the wife of the star of the movie and the girlfriend of the second male lead in the movie, but that is where the Hollywood trope ends. Patricia Arquette understood the meal she had been served, and she ate up every opportunity she was given in that script. She created two diametrically opposed characters who are wrapped in completely different mysteries. She is forced at gunpoint to strip in front of Mr. Eddy and a room full of his bodyguards and then walk over and kneel in front of him. While it is a scary but ultimately thrilling activity for the character of Alice, who, remember, is an avatar from the mind of a misogynist, it can't be forgotten that actress Patricia Arquette had to strip with a gun pointed to her head in front of actor Robert Loggia, a team of background actors, and the crew of the film. Arquette commands power throughout this scene but admitted in an interview back in 1997 that she would cry between takes. The nerves of the actress are nowhere on screen. Conversely, her character of Renee is cloaked in fear for her entire stint in the movie. If Arquette plays her as too much of a victim, the audience will start to suspect Fred too soon. She magnificently walks this tightrope of indifference and fear, keeping viewers guessing at what is really going on in the Madison house. At the hands of a lesser actress, the character of Renee could have destroyed the entire feel of the movie. Arquette understood her job and performed it to perfection.

When your career is as prolific as Arquette's is, it's hard to give her kudos for every home run performance in her catalog. She won an Oscar for *Boyhood*. She will always be thought of as being "so cool" for creating the first female character written by Quentin Tarantino as Alabama Whitman in *True Romance*. In 2022, she created a disturbing boss who not only terrorizes her employee at work but lives next door to him after work in the current Apple TV series *Severance*. She has done so much top-notch work that it is easy to forget what she did in *Lost Highway*. With all that being said, I wondered if she had forgotten it too. Who could blame her? It was a difficult shoot, a movie that was panned, and had been twenty-five years. In reaching out to the entire cast, I had the least hope of getting an Arquette interview. How foolish of me. She was the first person to say yes. She knew her character(s) like she was still on the set of the film. I was able to speak with her over the phone for a thirty-minute interview in the summer of 2022. It was an honor and a privilege to discuss her exquisite work in the film, and I am really proud of myself for resisting the urge to say to her, "You're so cool." But she sure as hell is.

Scott Ryan: You said in an interview from 1997 that it would take a decade for audiences to catch up to *Lost Highway*. It's been twenty-five years. Did they catch up yet?

Patricia Arquette: I don't know. Honestly, it's still ahead of its time even looking at it now. I think that it does have a core audience that has really appreciated this movie for twenty-five years and are still befuddled, surprised, and excited by this material. It's kind of ageless because if you are a person with a certain kind of sensibility, this movie will always be relevant to you.

Ryan: Where were you in your career when you decided to make *Lost Highway*?

Arquette: That's a good question. I will have to IMDb me.

[*The phone goes dead. Her assistant calls me back.*]

Arquette: Hi, Scott.

Ryan: I didn't think *that* would be the question that would make you hang up on me.

Arquette: GOODBYE, SCOTT! [Laughs.] I think I had done *Flirting with Disaster* before *Lost Highway*. I had always loved movies that were a little bit less popular. I did *The Indian Runner*. A lot of things I had done were more mainstream because I was blonde, blah, blah, blah. I had always loved David Lynch's movies and films that were a little more experimental and artistic, so I was really excited to get a chance to do it. It was really challenging for me because there was a lot of nudity in it, and I was personally really phobic about nudity to a strange extent, and I felt it would maybe help me tackle my demons.

Ryan: I have a quote from you that you cried in between takes and one time you even called David Lynch "Satan."

Arquette: Oh yeah, well, I did, and he said, "Hey, you read the script." And I don't think he appreciated being called Satan. [Laughs.] And I don't really think David is Satan, but these guys were kind of weird in this group scene, and they were acting weird and being weird. So when I said that to David, he was like, "What's going on?" I said, "These guys are not being appropriate." Not so much in the scene as outside the scene or before the scene. I don't know. It wasn't necessarily the scene. So David took them all aside and had a chat with them. [Laughs.] When I came back in, they were all *very* professional.

Ryan: The power that you have when you have a gun to your head and Mr. Eddy is forcing you to do something you don't want to do, the fact that, as an actress, the elements of that moment are a phobia for you—it doesn't come across on screen. How did you do that?

Alice has a gun to her head, but Patricia felt the same pressure. Photo courtesy of Ciby 2000/Criterion

Arquette: That is part of what acting is. It's figuring out what someone else's survival mechanisms are. How they incorporate that into their life. How *they* think!

Ryan: I would have never known that you were feeling that way; you display such power. Compare and contrast that scene with the fight scene with James Gandolfini in *True Romance.*

Arquette: The *True Romance* scene we shot for days on end. I worked with my acting teacher at the time, Roy London. The concept behind that scene, which we worked out, was that Alabama was kind of stalling. And it was there in the material. She was waiting for her boyfriend to come save her, and trying to charm him, and use all these survival mechanisms she had to bide time for her boyfriend to come back. At a certain point she realized he wasn't going to come back in time. Something in her rose up. At the beginning of the scene he says, "The first time I killed someone I threw up." You change after you kill someone. By the end of the scene, she has killed someone, and she is no longer the same.

Ryan: The power that you bring to characters has been inspiring.

Patricia Arquette had plenty of practice displaying power on screen after filming this fight scene with James Gandolfini in *True Romance.* Photo courtesy of Warner Bros. Pictures

Your character in *Lost Highway* says, "You'll never have me." That has become such an important line for so many female Lynch fans. I don't know if you know the importance of that line for the fans who go to David Lynch for that kind of strength in his female characters. Did you feel any pressure for how you'd deliver that line? Did you know it would become iconic?

Arquette: I didn't, but I do think it is central to the core. Part of what is incredible about working with David is, as the director, he doesn't tell you that it is central. Some directors really want to micromanage your every feeling, glance, and everything. You feel like a puppet. David is not like that. He has a lot of strict boundaries, as far as the meter of the scene. He is very musical. If I'd ask him, "Am I playing two people or one?" He would say, "Well, what do you think, Patrish?" And I'd say, "Am I dead or a ghost? What am I? [Laughs.] Am I a hallucination?" He would just say, "What do you think, Patrish?"

What I ended up deciding for myself was that Fred is the modern man, so he didn't want to see himself like this misogynist monster. But it was inside of him. He touched her car when he came home to see if she'd been out. They were like two panthers watching each other. She was kind of trying to starve him out to get him to leave. Then he transforms and he's a beautiful young man and she needs him again. Now she is different this time. She wants him and he's young and he is virile. They are falling in love and having sex all the time, and its great. Then the same thing happens, and she has to be a whore/nightmare. So to me, it's like looking at women through the eyes of a misogynist. Even his fantasies will go wrong. Everything will go wrong because he REALLY can't be open. He really can never feel safe, and it always has to be somebody else's fault. I know David wrote this during the O. J. Simpson trial, and O. J. was all [said in a childlike voice], "I'm innocent. I'm innocent. I'm innocent" to a point where you started to wonder, "Does he even believe he is innocent? Maybe he actually thinks he is innocent. Has he even convinced himself at this point?"

So to me, that line, "You'll never have me," goes to the core of his fear. It's his worst nightmare. No matter what woman you have, they are gonna turn out to be a rotten liar, a cheater, and fucking everyone, and "you'll *never* have me."

Ryan: Love that answer. Tell me about the color schemes for both characters. How did color help you with these two characters?

Arquette: I was archetypically looking at these characters even in a larger sense than Fred and his subconscious misogyny. I was looking at them in the world's misogyny. The fables we hear about bad women throughout time. I modeled one on Salome and one on Jezebel. One to be light, and one to be dark. I thought, "OK, well, maybe I'll model this one's hair on Bettie Page." It was shocking. I showed David that and he was like, "Who is this?" I said, "There is no way you don't know who Bettie Page is?" Anyway, he didn't know who she was, but

Patricia Arquette created two sides of a woman.
Photos courtesy of Ciby 2000

he dug it. We went for that for Renee. Alice was kind of younger and brighter colored. With Renee, we were using dark-colored lipstick and nails. With Alice, we had more brightly colored nails. Renee is a little more elegant. Alice was a little younger and trashier.

Ryan: I noticed your nails change colors. Is there anything to be learned from that?

Arquette: I remember there was a scene where we put on these green nails. I think Alice is crying in bed with Pete, and I am gesturing with my hands and David was like, "Oh my God, those nails, they are zinging. Solid gold, Dark Cat."

Ryan: What is it like to be directed by David Lynch?

Arquette: We had this hallway tracking shot, and in this tracking shot, you are supposed to stay a certain distance behind the camera. The camera is pulling in front of you, and you are supposed to kind of walk whatever it is, three feet, behind it. If you get closer, it gets blurry inside the minimum focus of the camera. So I am walking down the hallway, and David says, "Cut, print." Then the camera department says, "Hold on. It was inside focus. Part of it is blurry." He said, "Great. Print it. I want to see what that looks like." He always was open to accidents being art. He thought, "Good because audiences need to get used to different kinds of focuses and non-focus. I want to see what that looks like." He was open to the crew coming up with ideas for things. David is an incredible, genius filmmaker. Once in a lifetime—they don't make them like that. He broke the mold. I am so lucky, so, so lucky to have had a chance to work with such an incredible genius as David Lynch.

Ryan: You are incredible in the movie. The two characters you crafted are so different. It had to be fun to have such a meaty roll at such a young age.

Arquette: Oh yeah. I mean, it was terrifying. But totally exciting. I didn't want to drop the ball or let anyone down. That is kind of my own chemistry. My own problems. [Laughs.] Too much information?

Ryan: Not at all. That is what makes you a good artist. If you weren't afraid, what would be the point of doing it?

Arquette: I imagine some actors are like egomaniac monsters; not a lot, but there are some of those. That is really fascinating too. With Alice, in a way, she is a damsel in distress, and then in another way she is veracious.

Ryan: Any stories about working with Robert Blake as the Mystery Man?

Arquette: Robert Blake kept telling me these kinds of *Baretta* stories and using these *Baretta* euphemisms and catchphrases. It was just weird. He kept telling me about this Bonny [Lee Bakley] and what an angel she was, and that is the woman who ended up dying. I don't know. It was just too weird. He was kind of playing, to me, Satan. Also, really he is playing Fred's interior true self, the monster that does hate women in the flesh. So when he is saying, "I'm in your house," it's the house of your body. It's in your own self. "I'm in your house. I'm in you." Anyway, look, I need to make answers for myself to understand the story, to some extent, to be able to give myself over to it. It is really only *Lost Highway* and *Severance* where I felt like, "Woah, where am I? What am I doing?"

Ryan: I love that show. It's killing me to not pound you with questions about *Severance*.

Arquette: I'm not telling you anything! I am superpleased to be on it. I'm really pleased to be an actress who has been in these two projects that are very nebulous, hard to figure out, terrifying, experimental, and artistic. I just feel very lucky to be in this place where I had the opportunity in these different periods of my life to be in two things that terrified me so much. I am kind of trying to figure them out and wrestling with them. I know it sounds weird, and it's not always easy.

Ryan: No, it makes sense. I can't imagine anyone else playing your part in *Severance*. I am obsessed with it. There is gonna be a Season 2, right?

Arquette: Yes, there is.

Ryan: Good, otherwise I am throwing my Apple TV out the door.

Arquette: [Laughs.]

Ryan: Tell me something about *True Romance*. What is your strongest memory of making that film?

Arquette: I loved director Tony Scott so much. I can't tell you how much he gave to me. I grew up unaware, but as a girl in the world, I would try to appease people and make sure they were OK. I'd try to have my mind, choices, and thoughts but also appease others too because they didn't always like that or agree with me. So how could I get them to see my point of view? It was a lot of work. When I showed up on *True Romance*, it was like Tony was this idealist dad for a girl. Every idea I had, he said, "Great idea. Bama's got an idea. Let's do this." I never had someone say "Yes, yes, yes, yes" all the way down the line. I had done *True Romance* before I had done *Lost Highway*. So he really kind of taught me to listen to my instincts and that they weren't bad. It wasn't always going to be scary for someone to hear your ideas; maybe they were really good. There was only one time that he said, "I don't know about that idea." I said, "OK, that is cool. Let's do it your way." Then he said, "I think Bama's right, let's do it her way." Meanwhile, every idea that Christian Slater came up with Tony, would say, "That is a terrible idea." Christian was like, "What the fuck, man?" That changed my life. The relationship a director can have with an actor can really change everything forever for you, for good or for bad.

Ryan: I can't watch *True Romance* without watching Lynch's *Wild at Heart*. They go together so perfectly. Do you see a connection between the films?

Arquette: Sure. I mean, there is a lot of the same kind of costumey thing. There is a lot of crossover between Nic Cage and Christian's character visually—even Laura Dern's character and mine. There is a poppiness, kind of a bubblegum, coolness thing going on. There are also two lovers on the road. Sure, I can see that. It's funny, because for so long the stories were about buddy movies, and they were about two guys. These couples aren't buddies; they are lovers. But it was a couple. There weren't a lot of those before these films.

Ryan: When you think of the best romantic film couples, you feel that Alabama loves Clarence so much. The same way that Lula loves Sailor so much. It's because they do these crazy things together. I think *True Romance* is one of the best love stories ever told. It is up there with *The Way We Were*.

Lula and Sailor from Lynch's *Wild at Heart*.
Photo courtesy of Polygram

Arquette: The thing about it is that in a lot of relationships, they don't give someone else the benefit of the doubt, and we don't even think of it as the way relationships work. But Bama supports Clarence except for when he gets the stuff from the pimp. They are pretty much supporting each other—in who they are and how they see the world and the choices each other is making—and that is what doesn't happen in a lot of relationships. They don't give them the benefit of the doubt, and they don't have good will toward each other.

Ryan: Like when she is crying after he kills the pimp and then she says she is crying because it was the sweetest thing anyone ever did for her.

Arquette: That was actually one of the hardest scenes for me, because I was like, "Shit, man, she is saying all this to a dude who just killed somebody?" Yes, the pimp was a bad guy, but, like, whoa. My acting teacher helped with this. This isn't something you are going to see in the movie, but he said, "But how scary must this be to be in a room with someone who just killed someone who is capable of killing someone? What are you gonna say, 'What the fuck did you do?' What if he kills you too?" Of course it is a survival mechanism. I, as the actress, had a hard time, and the audience doesn't know that, Clarence doesn't know that, and Bama may not even know that, but that is part of what is playing underneath the scene. "OK, you are a murderer, wow, OK. How do I survive this moment?"

Ryan: I love that; that is such a great way to look at that scene. Turning back to *Lost Highway*, when Fred says, "I like to remember things my own way." How do you remember *Lost Highway* twenty-five years later in your own way?

Arquette: I am lucky that I came up at a time before you Instagrammed every meal and what you wore. There were no tracking devices. But I think it is nice to see a movie and then let it reflect back on you. It's nice to have a memory of an experience and not have it fully documented everywhere to double-check yourself. It is where I was at that moment in my life. It's interesting being an actor because you have your experience in front of the camera, and you have it behind the camera with the crew and everyone: David, the camera department, props, your dressing room, craft service people, and all these other things. You are all making something together. Looking back on *Lost Highway*, it was a real work of art. I am so grateful to be part of that. I got to work with David Lynch, Bill Pullman, and all these wonderful people.

Ryan: Did you conquer your phobia and fears?

Arquette: No. [Laughs.] Not at all. Momentarily I did, and I do think it was the right choice. I didn't want to limit myself by other survival mechanisms women might have in the world. It was the first time I got to play a *monster*, even though it is a monster made up in someone's mind. It was the first time I got to play a bad person. Or a scary person, like I play in *Severance*. It was my first. Girls don't get to play much, especially in the nineties and being a blonde and being that young age. There were very few parts like that. It was great.

***

I didn't say it to her on the phone, but I'll say it here: Patricia Arquette, you're so cool.

CHAPTER 5
DEEPAK NAYAR

Deepak has been in the right place at the right time for most of his life. His story, which I'll let him tell, is pretty incredible. It's a true Hollywood story and actually sounds a lot like the plot of *Mulholland Dr.* But he just wasn't quite in the right spot for me. While I am beyond thrilled to have him in this book because he is one of the *Lost Highway* producers (along with Mary Sweeney and Tom Sternberg), it kind of kills me that I didn't have him in my last book. He was the first AD (assistant director) on *Fire Walk With Me* and has some wonderful stories that would have fit perfectly in *Fire Walk With Me: Your Laura Disappeared.* Sticking to the idea that plot has no importance to Lynch fans, I let those stories be told in this book. Think of it as an Easter egg for those Lynch fans who love all his work. Nayar is an amazing storyteller. He doesn't answer questions, he has yarns to spin. You will feel his joy permeating the stories he tells about the good old days with his dear friend. Enjoy the producer of the film, a wonderful storyteller, and David Lynch's friend, Deepak Nayar.

Scott Ryan: How did David Lynch come into your life?

Deepak Nayar: David Lynch came into my life because I was his driver on the pilot of *Twin Peaks.* I met him when I was sitting at

Propaganda Films. I went up to Seattle and Snoqualmie and was his driver. Then I became a second second AD on *Twin Peaks*, then second AD, then I was the first AD on the feature film *Fire Walk With Me*. David was responsible for me becoming a producer. I have *a lot* to thank him for in life.

Ryan: That is quite a journey from driver to producer. That is like a Hollywood dream.

Nayar: Yes. I have been a producer for thirty years. I have produced maybe seventy-five films and television series. I do real estate, music publishing; I have a distribution company in India. I have lots of businesses. So David was responsible for that. When I was working as a first AD on *Twin Peaks*, his agent Tony Krantz, who was doing *On the Air*—ABC had picked up the series—Tony asked David, "Who do you want to be the line producer for *On the Air*?" David pointed to me, and that was it.

Ryan: What did you think of *On the Air* and the way ABC treated it?

Nayar: The thing about working with David Lynch is that you have to go with the flow of what he is trying to do. Sometimes you get it, and sometimes you don't. The times you don't get it, you say, "What was this all about?" But *On the Air* was a very clever series. To some degree, you can see traces of it in Disney's *WandaVision*. I don't think people got it. I also produced *Hotel Room* with David for HBO, and I don't think people got that either. The concept was very interesting—a hotel room where guests have stayed over the years. What would the walls say if they could talk? What would their stories be?

Ryan: I love the Alicia Witt episode of *Hotel Room*.

Nayar: He is an amazing director and manages to get performances out of these actors that nobody else can get. Look at all the talent that has worked with him and what they end up doing with him. He has an uncanny ability to do that. It is not like he is doing take after

A fan spins above Nicolas Cage and Laura Dern in *Wild at Heart*.
Photo courtesy of Universal Pictures

take. I remember I was a second AD on *Wild at Heart* working on the shot of Sailor and Lula looking through the fan from the bed, and David did just two takes and the whole thing was done. Everybody was panicking. One of the things you enjoy working with David is that you have no clue how your day is going to go. It is so much fun to be with him. You just have no idea what is going to happen, and that is so wonderful every day. He never loses his temper. I would always say, "David, you have fallen behind." He would say, "Should I stop shooting? Do you think we will catch up?" [Laughs.] I was only a second on *Wild at Heart*. We had spent three-quarters of the day rehearsing; we hadn't got a single shot. It was just a two- or three-page scene. Then he does these three shots. One a master, change the lens, change the lens, and then he does two takes and now we are early! Who the hell would know that? One moment you are thinking this is going to be a long day and the other moment you are thinking, "Shit, we wrapped early."

On *Lost Highway*, there was a shot of a cigarette burning. He wanted to see the entire cigarette burn without the ash falling. [Laughs.] Oh my God, that was the first shot of the day, and now hours go by because the ash would fall down. The entire crew is thinking, "How the hell do we get out of this thing?" because David is not moving forward. Everyone had their own scheme on how to keep this thing burning. Eventually we did get the shot. But it wasn't like you were pissed off. It became a challenge. Everybody had an idea. "We'll put a little thing in the cigarette . . ." Look, I have now produced many movies, but you remember certain key things and you think, "That is madness, complete madness, to have sixty people trying to figure out how to keep an ash from falling." You remember these things so vividly.

That is the beauty of working with David Lynch. One day he showed up late. I said, "David, what happened?" David's initials are DKL, and if he ever saw a license plate that had DKL, you can forget about him showing up on time. He was going to follow the car, and that is what happened. Craig MacLachlan, Kyle's brother, was David's driver. I said," What the fuck? Why are you late?" He said, "You have no idea. We were just following cars."

Ryan: One of the famous scenes in *Lost Highway* is the tailgating scene. Do you know where that came from?

Nayar: I was working with David at our offices. He was driving the truck, and there was a guy who was tailgating. And this guy was going left and right, and David said, "You know what I want to do? I want to let him pass and then take out a gun." And you know that scene is in *Lost Highway*. Robert Loggia does that. That was because something like that happened to David, and he was so pissed off at that guy and he translated that sequence into the movie.

We were shooting a sequence that didn't end up in the movie. Balthazar Getty comes up on a motorcycle into a diner, and then he leaves from there. The sequence proceeding the diner, everything was dry. Peter Deming had lit up the entire street. We had blocked everything off, and we had all these fancy cars that go up and down. It was a big sequence, and we had taken over this diner for a night shoot. But at five thirty in the evening, Peter Deming called me and said, "You better get out here." I said, "What happened?" He said, "It's pouring with rain here. What are we gonna do? Can we move the sequence inside?" I said, "I'll call David." So I called David up and said, "It's raining." He said, "It's not raining here." [Laughs.] I said, "Well, it is certainly raining there, and it's a night sequence and we cannot shoot outside continuity-wise. Can we move this inside?" He said, "Nope, Hotshot. We are gonna shoot outside. Get me two hoses and two boys and two girls and connect the hoses to a water pipe, and we are going to shoot outside."

I went to the set and told Peter [Deming] that we are going to shoot outside. Peter looked at me like I was a mad person. I said, "Don't look at me. I have no fucking clue what he wants to do." None of us have any clue what he is doing anyway. You just have to go with it. David arrived and asked if we had the hoses. He gathered us around and said, "Here is what we are going to do. Get the guys to take off their shirts and give them the hoses and tell them to squirt water at these girls." So the opening shot was of them doing that. You saw the water on the street. So the rain doesn't look like rain; it looks like these people were having fun with water outside. I thought, "What a brilliant solution." He was always an amazing last minute thinker who would make changes. If he genuinely had a problem, he would find a solution. When you make these movies, there are many directors that will never make a compromise. He wouldn't just compromise;

The deleted hose scenes
Photos courtesy of Fine Cut
Presentations

he would find a solution where you just sit back and say, "That is fantastic."

Ryan: What did you think of the script the first time you read it?

Nayar: David called me up at ten at night and said, "What are you doing? I am giving a script to William. It will take him five minutes to get to his car. He will get in his car at 10:05. Then he is going to drive from my house to your house. That will take him fifteen minutes. Give him an extra five for traffic. Now it is 10:25. At 10:27, he is going to knock on your door and hand you a script. It will take you two hours to read it. I will call you at 12:30 a.m." Basically telling me to sit down and read it. He called me and asked what I thought. I said, "I don't understand it at all." He said, "Fantastic. Let's make the movie now."

Ryan: Do you think you have to understand a movie to produce it?

Nayar: You make a choice when you decide to produce a movie with a director like David Lynch. You want to support his vision. The kind of movie David makes, there is nobody in front of him and nobody behind him. Others have tried to make similar kinds of movies, but it just doesn't work. My view has always been that if I wanted to have a creative thought process of that nature to understand and try to do it, then I should be a director myself. I have worked with Jane Campion, Paul Schrader. My position was always to support their vision. When you are getting involved with David Lynch, you are there to support him. Once he showed me the cut, I said, "The Balthazar story, to me, needs to be cut down." It was just Mary Sweeney, David, and me watching it. Mary was looking at me, like, "Are you sure you want to say that?" I had such a cool relationship with him that it didn't matter. He said, "Deepak, you are right." I said, "That is a scary thought if I am beginning to think like you. I don't want to do that." [Laughs.]

Ryan: How much longer was Balthazar's story?

Nayar: It was quite a bit longer. It's a very trippy affair. My view about *Lost Highway* is that it is one of his very cool films. You have to see it a few times before you understand it. The actual story only plays for just four or five minutes. The rest of it is just a lot of schizophrenic things. Fred knows the police are coming after him, and he just tries to run away from them. The beginning is the end of the movie. He gives you hints. He shows you the photographs. It's just the journey. Much of what I loved about working with David is that he takes a simple thing, and then it's the journey that you go on with him that is phenomenal. *Lost Highway* is a completely amazing journey about what a schizophrenic thinks.

Ryan: Patricia talked about her phobia of doing nude scenes. What was that sensitivity like for you as a producer to calm her?

Nayar: It is one of her best performances. It was also one of Bill Pullman's best performances. Her phobia did not rise to my level. David seemed to sort it out. To make sure that she was comfortable, we had standard operating procedures. Scott Cameron would close up the set and get everyone out. We didn't rush. We had to make our days for the overall production, but these scenes took longer. There usually are a bunch of crew people standing there to make any changes. My view was always clear everyone, lock the set up, and then everyone comes back in after. So there is always a time loss between takes. Because if you have to make an adjustment, a gaffer has to come back in. We also didn't use a monitor. You try to make it as comfortable as possible. If you do it by the book, it takes time because the minutes are adding up. You are going to lose a couple of hours in the day, but you make a choice that you want your talent to be very comfortable.

Ryan: What Lynch gets out of actresses is incredible. Why is he so good at creating these performances?

Nayar: He understands the characters very well. He tends to have written them. He also does a lot of rehearsal. Until he gets the mood, he just doesn't care about "Let's get the shot." He wants to get the level of performance in his rehearsal to a level where he thinks he has brought these actors into the frame of mind that they need to be in in order to perform it. Sometimes he would do hours of rehearsal, then they would go back to makeup, and they would do several hours of rehearsal again because he would feel they have gone out of character. And when he would "take a five," *everybody* is gone. I mean, no matter who you were. Only the first AD and the script supervisor. No DP, no production; everybody is gone. I only know because I was a first AD, and I would just sit in the corner and try not to make any eye contact. You sit there in a sort of nonexistence. You are only there in case he needs something. He tries to have a chat. He doesn't like to do too many takes. He *knows* what he wants.

On *Lost Highway*, I remember we were in this big house where they have the photographs. Not the opening sequence house; the house that the FBI guys come in. There was a scene with Bill Pullman. It was the last day we had the house. The house cost us a lot of money, and we weren't coming back there at all. He knew we had to finish the sequence. Maybe it was the pressure of that, or maybe he was tired. Take one. Take two. Take three. Take four. Take fifteen. Take twenty. Oh my God. I had never seen David go to that many takes for an actor. Bill was also getting frustrated. He didn't know what to give him. Bill was getting tired. We were going late into the night. I can't remember, at around eighteen I walked up to him and said, "I think we should go home. Everyone seems tired." He said, "But what about that we were supposed to finish today?" I said, "We will finish it later. We'll come back tomorrow. No big deal. So what? Let's just go home." So the next day, I didn't bring the entire crew there. We took a small crew up there. He did one take, and we were out. We were out in an hour and a half.

I used to love to bet him one dollar as to how many takes he was going to do. The dollar was an honorable bet. On *Fire Walk With Me*, Ron Garcia, Cori Glazer, David, and myself were driving to the set on a Friday. He asked me, "What time are we going to finish on Saturday?" I said, "David, ask me what time we are going to finish on Sunday morning." He said, "That's bullshit." So Cori goes through the call sheet and all the scenes that were left to film. David said, "We are going to finish at midnight on Saturday." I said, "David, I don't want to be disrespectful, but let me explain to you how shooting works. We are heading to the set right now on a Friday evening at six o'clock. We will finish around Saturday at six in the morning. I have to give a full twelve-hour turnaround to the actors. The earliest call would be 7:00 p.m. on Saturday, and you are telling me that you are going to finish all of this in four or five hours?" He pauses and thinks and says, "YES!" I said, "This calls for a bet." He said, "You are on, Rock Star." So we bet, but this time it was for twenty dollars, which was a lot, since we normally bet only one dollar.

At two thirty in the afternoon, Craig MacLachlan called and said, "David wants to talk to you." He said, "Where are you?" I said, "David, I am in my room. I just woke up." He said, "I'll see you in an hour. Let's have something to eat." I come down and there is Ron, Cori, and Craig. They are looking at me like, "What the fuck?" I have no idea. David said, "Let's go through everything we are going to do." We sat there till 5:30 p.m., and he said, "Let's go to the set." I said, "David, the call is to leave the hotel at 6:30 p.m. We will be the first ones to arrive." We left. The thing you have to understand—there is so much enjoyment when you work with David. So none of this is bad.

Sheryl Lee brings Laura Palmer to life in *Fire Walk With Me*.
Photo courtesy of Janus Films

It is more like, "What the fuck is going to happen?" Nobody is pissed off that they went to bed at 7:00 a.m. and are now headed to the set early. On the drive to the set, he said to Craig MacLachlan, "Can you step on the gas? I saw a cyclist overtake us." We arrived at the set; we were the first ones there. There was not even a single teamster. There was nothing to do but laugh. The teamster showed up and he said, "Am I late?" I told him it's fine.

David said to Ron, "Let's put the camera together." Ron said, "I haven't put a camera together in years. I don't know how to do that." The first AC [assistant camera] did it. Now the word filtered out that there is something going on between Deepak and David Lynch. Everyone is excited. The crew splits up into three crews: one prelighting, one shooting, and one wrapping up. At two minutes to midnight, he looked at me and said, "Do you want to call it a wrap or shall I?" I said, "The honor is all yours." I took out twenty dollars and gave it to David. Then I turned to Gregg Feinberg, who was the producer, and held out my hands, and he gave me a hundred dollars. David was SO MAD at me. He said, "You bet against yourself?" I said, "David, I am not an idiot. You are the director." He announced to everyone, "Deepak is going to buy drinks when we get back to the hotel." He made sure I burnt through that hundred dollars. [Laughs.]

Ryan: Oh my, that is a crazy story. Do you have any idea what scenes you were shooting that night?

Nayar: It was with Sheryl Lee. I know because Sheryl had to do two sequences and had to do a wardrobe change. So we finished the first sequence, and I said, "OK, Sheryl. Go back to the trailer and change." David Looked at me and said, "Where are you sending her?" I said, "I am sending her to change wardrobe." He said, "She's going to go all the way to the trailer and then change and then come back? I see how you are wasting my time. No, that is not going to happen. Grips, turn around, make a circle. Sheryl, change in there." He made her change right there on the fucking spot, surrounded by grips. It was hilarious. But I can't remember the sequence. Scott, you have to understand this is going back so many years.

Ryan: I get it. It would just be fun to know as a fan what scene it was. Any other *Fire Walk With Me* stories?

Nayar: On *Fire Walk With Me*, we were going to the set and David said, "Stop the car. See that woman over there? Go get her name and number." I said, "For what?" He said, "I don't know. Just get it." I got her number. Then later that day, he said, "You know that lady? She's in the next shot." I said, "What do you mean she is in the next shot?" He said, "Harry Dean Stanton is standing here, and then she will come in and say, 'Where's my hot water?' Then she goes." I said, "No, we can't do that right now. We can shoot her later in the day." Now I am trying to find her and get her right away. And she is in the movie.

Ryan: I love the Hot Water Lady. It's exciting to know where she came from. Tell me about filming the Madison house, which was Lynch's house.

We finally know where this woman came from in *Fire Walk With Me*.
Photo courtesy of New Line Cinema

Nayar: The house we shot in wasn't his house; it was next to it. Once he had bought the house, he had Patty Norris construct the house the way he wanted it. You could only do that if you owned the property.

Ryan: Did that save you money?

Nayar: Yes. David likes to act and react. If you have worked with him, you keep that in mind. The crew that works with him understand that is what is going to happen. Part of the charm was always what is the curveball that he is going to throw at you that you haven't thought of? For me, it was a lot easier being a producer with him.

Ryan: Any changes from the script that you remember?

Nayar: When you have a production meeting, you have a script and a read through. David will come in and say, "Look down below, you have a trash can. Throw that script in the trash can. Thank you, the production meeting has ended." There you go. What does that tell you? What are you talking about the script for? That is for normal people. You are working with David; you have to go with the flow.

Ryan: How was filming out in the desert?

Nayar was not a big fan of filming in the cold Death Valley.
Photo courtesy of Ciby 2000

Nayar: We were shooting in Death Valley. David knew that I hated the cold. He would make a point to come up with an excuse that I would have to come out of the trailer and hang out with him and be miserable. He would love it. I would ask him, "Is there a real reason I am out here?" He would say, "Let me just finish the shot. Do you want me to tell you everything right now or make the movie?" [Laughs.] It was wonderful. I would tell him, "You are going to go off to sleep, but that doesn't mean my work is finished. You just think it is. Some of us have to work for a living." He used to ask for a doughnut. You could see his energy was fading away. I would ask if he wanted a half load or a full load, being a half a doughnut or a full doughnut. Then we would get him a half load and a coffee to keep him going.

Ryan: The movie didn't do well at the box office. How did you feel personally at the way it was received?

Nayar: I think it got caught in the minutiae of distribution. I think *Lost Highway* is one of his best movies. Maybe I am biased about it. Siskel and Ebert didn't understand David. People want to pigeonhole him into something. The more you want to pigeonhole him, the more he wants to rebel against it. Sometimes that is good and sometimes that is bad. You don't want to come see a David Lynch movie where everything is wrapped up. He wants you to think, to step outside of yourself. Everything is not going to be cookie cutter. Not that you just have a good time. For that, go see a popcorn movie. If you want to see cinema, you want to ask, "What the fuck is that?" You have to watch *Lost Highway* three times to understand what he has to say.

Ryan: Twenty-five years later, it played in theaters again. How did that make you feel?

Nayar: It makes me feel very proud. Since we are now in the time of Marvel movies, I am not sure how many people will want to see it. This generation has not grown up with that kind of cinema, and I don't know if they will accept it. I think it is one of David's best. The first time is such a ride, you say, "What? What did I see?" But then the second time, you say, "Oh, I missed that." It is a very simple movie but told in a complex way. That is the beauty of that movie. It is phenomenal in how he tells a story. Fred says, "I like to remember things my way." That is what David is putting on the screen. Fred's version of what it is. We are so caught up in wanting to watch linear stories and wanting to understand it all, but if something is out of the ordinary, where you actually have to step back and marvel at what has been done, that requires more than watching a movie and saying it's cool.

Ryan: What will you remember most from your time with David Lynch?

Nayar: People ask me what it is like to work with David Lynch, but I have no clue. He is just an amazing person. I will always be extremely thankful, and I am so happy that Sabrina Sutherland is working with him now. She was my coordinator on *Twin Peaks*. When I did *On the Air*, I brought her with me. On *Lost Highway*, she was with me as my production manager. She understands him just as well. It is OK I am not there, but part of me is there with him because Sabrina was with me all those years. She is a very, very nice person. I have so much respect and love for David. My relationship with him and what I have managed to achieve from starting as his driver to where I have now financed over seventy-five films and the amount of stuff I am doing, and it's all because he believed in me. Our paths separated after *Lost Highway*, but I admire him a lot, and I have a lot to thank him for.

CHAPTER 6
SABRINA S. SUTHERLAND

If you are a hardcore Lynch fan, it's hard to imagine a time when Sabrina Sutherland wasn't sitting right next to David Lynch. But, as you will read in this interview, it took a long time and a lot of work for Sutherland to finally call "Shotgun." Sutherland worked on *Twin Peaks* (Season 2), *On the Air*, *Hotel Room*, and has worked on every major Lynch project since *Lost Highway*. The amount of work she did in producing the eighteen hours of *Twin Peaks: The Return* is an achievement that very few producers in Hollywood can claim. But on *Lost Highway*, she was not THE producer. She was a production supervisor working under Deepak Nayar, whom she had worked under for all her prior projects. *Lost Highway* was the transitional project for her. She is now Lynch's right-hand woman, and she helps bring to life all of his visions. No one can think that is an easy job.

I have been very fortunate to have interviewed her many times over the past seven years. She has always been so kind and supportive of all my projects. I can say she is the *only* person I have ever interviewed who always purchases the products we make, be it magazines or books, whether she is a part of the project or not. As a small business owner, I truly appreciate that. But for me, as someone who studies human nature, it says so much about who she is as a person. She doesn't approach life feeling as if she is owed something. She cares about the world of Lynch and is a consumer of the art that is created from his world. As if it isn't evident, I am a big fan of hers and find her to be an honorable and very kind person. I hope readers will feel her professionalism and attention to detail in this interview. She had just finished working on the Criterion Blu-ray release of *Lost Highway* with David Lynch. It hadn't come out yet, so I was excited to hear how it would look. Since we live on different coasts, the only time we could find to do this interview required her to get up early to speak with me before her workday with Lynch began. Therefore, my first question had to be …

Scott Ryan: Have you been caffeinated?

Sabrina S. Sutherland: Believe it or not, I don't do that. I drink tea.

Ryan: And Lynch approves of that? I would think you would have to be downing some serious coffee, man.

Sutherland: I think David drinks enough for everybody!

Ryan: I actually drink decaf coffee, but if I was around him, I wouldn't admit to it and I'd do the caffeine.

Sutherland: I have no problem saying I don't want any. [Laughs.]

Ryan: Thanks for talking with me about *Lost Highway*.

Sutherland: My pleasure. To be honest, I think it was forgotten. It didn't do that well when it opened in the US. I think it's a great movie. It just hasn't been seen in a long time.

Ryan: I thought we would start in the present. Tell me about the 4K restoration and what that entails and why a movie needs one.

Sutherland: There are new technologies that come out. Back in 1995/96 when we did the film, David put all his thought into the technology of that time, but the print really hasn't been updated by

David until now. You can imagine how many new technologies there are from that time till now. We have worked with Criterion, and they have done wonderful work on everything that David has done. They really take care to make sure that it is something that is a work of art. It's not just putting something out to make money. They put care into it. They get the original negative and do a high-res scan so the film looks as good as possible. Then it gets cleaned up so there are no dust particles on it. *Lost Highway* changed the way David works in post with the lab. He had always used CFI, which is a laboratory. We are talking about film negative, not digital. When we were shooting *Lost Highway*, we were out in Death Valley, and there was a huge sandstorm, and I mean HUGE. We were on a dry lake bed in the night with the car headlights on Patricia and Balthazar. The dust in this dry lakebed was really fine, and all of a sudden there was a wall of dust. In the movie, it looks like it's a special effects kind of thing. It's all natural. The wind picked up, and all this dust flew. Dust got everywhere. The whole crew had to put on masks and went into a tent area. You couldn't breathe. We shut down until that wind stopped.

Ryan: So how does that dust not get on the 35 mm film?

Sutherland: Exactly. It did. It got into the camera, the film. We did have a lot of damage, for sure. The film went to CFI, and it was filled with dust. The person who dealt with the film said the best person to fix this was FotoKem. That is when David's relationship started with them. FotoKem took the film, and they had a special bath. I don't remember who did it, but they took the film and put it in warm water, and someone had to, frame by frame, clean the dust off of the negative. It was painstaking. The scan that Criterion did for this new release in 2022 still had that residue on the film, and it had to be cleaned off the negative. It was just the scenes out in Death Valley that had the dust on it, but it was still there.

Ryan: When Lynch finishes a movie, is there one original print that goes somewhere safe? Where has *Lost Highway* been all this time? Was it in a box in David Lynch's basement?

Sutherland: There is a negative that is stored by the distribution company. Whoever has control over the film has the cut negative. That is the prized possession and is put in storage to save. There are prints that are made that are shown in theaters, so you aren't showing the original film. Otherwise, you'd only be able to show it in one place, and it would be dangerous. Film breaks; it is delicate. Janus Films, which distributes the film, is focused on classics and restoration. That makes them the kings of the film world in terms of classics. They really respect film.

Ryan: I just saw all of Lynch's film in 35 mm at Daniel Knox's Lynch retrospective in Chicago. It really reenergized my love for 35 mm. It's the way film needs to be seen. How do you get that look on Blu-ray?

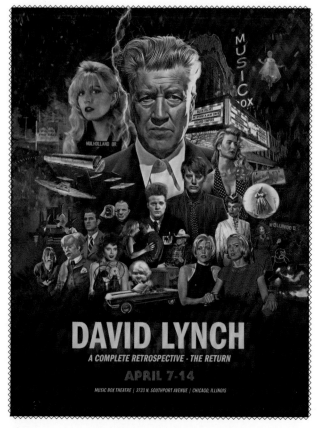

The poster for the Music Box's David Lynch event.
Poster by Sean Longmore

Sutherland: For me, I love film. I love theaters because there is a look that they try to replicate at home, but there is no way of making it exactly like film. Kodak film versus Fuji film has different looks or feels. Everything about film is different from digital. Companies have been trying to replicate that look as much as they can. It's getting closer, but you are never going to get it exactly. There is a difference between digital on your TV and film being played through a projector. Even projecting a digital piece through a projector is different. There may not be that big of a difference for those who aren't appreciative of film, but people who have a discerning eye can tell the difference.

Ryan: What is brought out in the new 4K print of *Lost Highway*?

Sutherland: It brings the best of the film to a digital form. So you have it as close to what the actual film was like in a digital form. The colors, the blacks, are as close to what the film is. There are some people who will always want to see film no matter what, but when we are talking about watching the film in your living room or in a theater that doesn't even have a film projector, this is as close as you are going to get.

Ryan: I saw *Lost Highway* for the first time on VHS and it looked horrible. It may be one of the worst transferred movies ever. Were you disappointed in the VHS, and why has it taken so long to get a good version?

Sutherland: I couldn't tell you why there hasn't been something done sooner. Look at any of the movies that are on the darker side from the nineties and then transferred to VHS; there was never any real care taken with these films. Especially a film like *Lost Highway*, which was something that was looked at like "This film is going to do really well," and then it didn't. But like a lot of David's films, it was ahead of the curve. He isn't really appreciated until years later. That is just kind of his MO. The general public doesn't embrace him immediately. Maybe now it would be different. But at the time, people were not sitting there waiting for the next David Lynch film. And it wasn't received very well. In the late nineties, people were doing other things. His look wasn't really appreciated. Film companies don't put more money into something that they lose money on. When it came time to redistribute films, that wasn't the first film that came up.

Ryan: I have *Lost Highway* on DVD from overseas and one in America. One is so lightened up that I can't even stand to watch it, then the other is so dark that I can't see anything. Why is it such a hard film to release properly?

Sutherland: I feel that this is a beautiful film. I love watching it. I hadn't gone back to this film since I saw it in the nineties. Seeing it now and seeing what David did to it by going frame by frame was super important. I fell in love with the film a lot.

Ryan: Why do you like it a lot?

Sutherland: Of course I like it because I worked on it. It brings back a lot of things from making it. When you are remastering something, it's not like you watch it one day and it's done. You see it over and over and go through it. Then you have to watch it again to make sure it is right. I don't even remember how many times we watched it. The first time we went through it, the digital imaging people, George Koran, Angelique Perez, Mike Brodersen, who work at FotoKem, are with us every day as we go through everything. George works so closely with David to make sure it looks like David wants it to look. The first time going through, we would stop and talk about what happened that day. David always has so many stories that are great to hear again and again. We were telling the stories in addition to doing the work. By the time we finished and went through the film a bunch of times, we end the project by watching it one last time. During that viewing, I was just watching the film as a film. I thought, "Wow, this really is a good film." It was like I hadn't worked on it.

Ryan: *Lost Highway* is my favorite Lynch film right now, not counting *Fire Walk With Me*, which to me is just part of *Twin Peaks* and doesn't count. It has grown on me the more I have seen it. I have a theory for why it's his most satisfying film to watch. I think it is because it has his strongest ending. It really ends well. Once Bill Pullman comes back, there is so much momentum in the story. Most Lynch endings have a mysterious vibe and leave you in an unsettled mood. *Lost Highway* has a firecracker ending. This is a David Lynch movie that ends in a car chase. That's pretty darn rare. What do you think of that theory?

Sutherland: [Laughs.]

Ryan: Let me guess? No comment?

Sutherland: For me, well … that's a great … insight. I don't know. It's something to think about for sure. It still isn't ending with something that ties it all together by any means.

Ryan: Well, we'd be disappointed if it did. We don't want *that*.

Sutherland: [Laughs.] No. I do feel this film, for me, is the most relatable, and I could totally see in my mind what the story is. The meaning of this story is so blatant to me. I recently told this story to David, and he swears it didn't happen, but I went up to David on the *Lost Highway* set, and you would never do this to David Lynch, right? Certainly not, but I went up and said, "Here is my opinion on what this film is about." I went on to tell him what I thought this story was. [Scott laughs.] I know. Am I right? And I was naive to do that, but I did. I swear to you at the time he said, "That sounds about right." That is what I heard. To me, he was validating my theory of what the movie was about. Now we are doing this remastering, and I am sitting there and I told him this. He said, "I never said that to you." I said, "Yes, you did." He said, "No, no, no. I never told you anything about that." I said, "You basically told me I was right." And he said, "No, I wouldn't have done that." So we now have an argument about that.

Ryan: Do you want to share what your theory of the film was?

Sutherland: NO. [Waits a beat. And then we both burst out laughing.]

Ryan: I didn't think so. When I interviewed Patricia Arquette, I was impressed with how much she understood that movie and her character.

Sutherland: She was incredible in this film. The first time Balthazar sees her and the Lou Reed song "Magic Moment" is playing—just looking at her—I'm dumbstruck. That is part way through the film already. You see her at the beginning with Bill Pullman, and she is drop dead gorgeous. Both characters are so different; the acting is incredible. She totally is underrated. I don't know why. I know she is a big star and is always talked about. But why didn't she become this megastar? Because she is so good in this film. She is smart, sexy, and everything else you can think of for the best kind of actress. Personally, it was a difficult shoot with her because she was under so much pressure doing these things. Plus, there was a lot of nudity, which for any actress is a lot of high tension. In preproduction before we started shooting the film, we shot those stag films. Anybody taking

Sutherland is a big fan of Arquette. Photo courtesy of Ciby 2000

their clothes off, man or women, in front of a group of people is very discerning. It's a difficult thing to do. Actors are usually insecure. They put themselves out there, but they are sensitive souls. I don't know how many people can be happy standing naked in front of thirty to fifty people and doing their job at the same time. It is a very difficult thing. I know that was an issue for her from the first day doing the stag films. They were done quite privately, but all of her nakedness is on film. You don't want people looking at them outside of the film. It was my job to make sure that these stag films never saw the light of day. I was just talking with David and said that I want to be sure that all of those films were destroyed, because that was the note. They were supposed to be destroyed after editing in 1995.

Ryan: I feel like her power as Alice is in every scene. She is never a victim.

Sutherland: That credit goes to Patricia, because she is a great actress. I think people underestimate her. You don't see any of her struggle in the performance. Alice is the person in charge all the way to the end. Those things for her were difficult, and my job at the time, production supervisor, was to make sure that everything was handled. Deepak, being the producer he is, would come to set, but then he would leave. So I was his eyes and ears and the person in charge on set when he wasn't around. It was difficult, because you needed to make sure she was going to be OK, and it was hard for her.

Ryan: Tell me about purchasing the house to shoot the film in.

Sutherland: A neighbor passed away, and David was able to buy the house because he knew them. It was a perfect house for the film. That house is now David's sound studio. It was the perfect place to build the long hallway that Bill Pullman walked into and completely dissolved into black. You can see the curtains now in the new restoration; not in every scene, but when the light is on it, you can see them. I remember Peter Deming [director of photography] saying, "David, Bill is just gonna disappear," and David said, "Exactly. I want it pitch-black." He just kept screaming, "Pitch black!" I felt for Peter because he wants to light it and make things look good and doesn't want people to think it was a mistake and not done purposefully. Peter, at that time, was super experimental.

There were several things that David and Peter experimented with. One of them was the idea that David wanted something out of focus, and when Peter went out of focus as much as he could, David said it wasn't enough. So Peter actually pulled the lens, and David said that was perfect. Did Scott Ressler tell you the Gary Busey story?

Ryan: Not yet. That is later on in the book.

Sutherland: I will let him tell it. It's a good one.

Ryan: What about Richard Pryor? Any stories from working with him?

Sutherland: Wasn't he great? That was so wonderful. He was ad-libbing a lot of that. He had MS and hadn't been working at all at that point. I don't even know how [casting director] Johanna Ray got him. He was incredibly funny. He was saying all kinds of stuff. David used one option, but there were many takes, and every time he said something different.

Ryan: It sounds like a fun shoot.

Sutherland: It was Bill Pullman's birthday while we were shooting in Death Valley. First we shot there, and then we came to LA for the rest of the shoot. It was a short shooting schedule. Death Valley was hysterical. We were there over a week, and there weren't a lot of places to stay. When we were filming the dry lake bed stuff, most of us were staying in Baker, California. A few of us who didn't have to worry about time constraints in getting to set, we all stayed at Buffalo Bill's Resort and Casino in Primm at the border of Nevada that had a roller coaster [The Desperado]. So we were shooting nights, and everyday I'd be awake all day because I would hear "AHHHHHHHH!" right outside my window. I was so mad at Deepak. But then towards the end of that shoot, we moved to be closer to the opera house where we shot the hotel scenes. So we moved to this other place, and there was a real fancy hotel and then a lesser place to stay. There were only two choices. I was lucky enough to stay at the fancy hotel with the talent. We are talking in the middle of nowhere. They had a bar there which was the only place you could go. The entire crew went to the bar after shooting. So we are talking from Saturday night to Sunday. I went to meet with Deepak, and he asked me to come with him. It turned out that Bill Pullman was having a birthday, and he had invited Deepak to this small gathering, and Deepak brought me. It was nice, but I felt like Bill Pullman was looking at me like, "What the fuck is she doing here?" [Laughs.] Because there were only six to eight people there. He was gracious and I was able to stay. We drank a lot of wine. David and Peter were there, and I don't remember who else was there. I felt uncomfortable because I knew I wasn't invited, but I had fun. Afterwards, we went to another party downstairs with the entire crew. We go down there and everybody is drunk. We had I don't know how many bottles of wine. All of sudden David is up on-stage playing bongos. Everyone was performing and it was hysterical. Balthazar had a T-shirt and David was talking to him and he tried to run away from him, and David grabbed the shirt and it stretched at least like thirty feet. It was like a cartoon. He had to come back. I don't know what it was made out of. But seriously, he got halfway out of the bar and the shirt was still being held by David. It was a crazy night.

Ryan: Now that is a deleted scene we all would like to see. Deepak mentioned a scene where Lynch wanted to film a cigarette burning all the way down. Do you remember that?

Sutherland: It was a pain in the ass. That is what it is day in and day out working with David. The actors and the crew want to please David. You want to be recognized. It's a weird relationship. I don't know what he has over people. You have everybody vying for his attention and approval. You feel a sense of accomplishment if he says "Aces." You feel like you are validated. That is the way it is for every show he works on. You want to be the person who comes up with the great idea.

Ryan: Your relationship with David is different today than it was on *Lost Highway*. Looking back, what would you tell that Sabrina working on the film?

Sutherland: I was talking about that with David when we watched *Lost Highway* again. At that time, Deepak was really who I was working for. With his producing style, he works mainly in the office. He is looking at the budget and working with accounting, so he wasn't on the set that much. I was that point person on set, so David would have to call me for things, and it's not that he was wincing, but he *was* wincing and cringing. He would ask, "You think I could get a techno crane?" I would hate to be the person that said, "No, sorry you can't do that because we can't afford it." There is always a way to make what he wants happen. That is what Deepak always did. That is what I try to do. You never want to say no to David. There were times where I would be on set and David would see me and say, "What's wrong?" I tried to avoid David's eyes when I was on set. If he saw me, he would cringe. It was really hard for me because I wanted to hang out and be there, but I had to make it so he couldn't see me. If he saw me, his attitude would change because he saw me as the person who had the purse strings. It was very difficult at that time for me working with David.

One time I was called when the toilet in the Madison house was backed up. I heard, "Sabrina, you got to get to the set because the toilet is backed up." I remember Scott Ressler asking, "Is she a plumber?" That was what I was on those sets. I was not an equal. I was the person that handled all the problems and the money. David didn't want to see me around. He liked me as a person and was friendly outside of shooting.

Ryan: Does it change on *The Straight Story* or *Mulholland Dr.*? Where did you cross the hump with him?

Sutherland: It started when we did a Citroën commercial. David asked me to produce the commercial. I went to the set. It was a two-day shoot. I told him, "I will sit behind you so that you don't have to see me because I know that I distract you, and you get worried when you see me." He acknowledged it at that time. He said, "When I see you, I think you are going to tell me that I can't do something." I realized that I was right in my thinking. Then after that, I said, "I have my chair, but I am gonna sit just a little bit behind you." Then, on *Twin Peaks: The Return*, I remember starting out sitting just behind him, but I think halfway through shooting he started pulling my chair up next to him. That is when we crossed that line. It was more on the latest *Twin Peaks*, so it took all that time.

Ryan: So it only took twenty years!

Sutherland: Exactly. It took that long to finally be OK with him for

Sutherland sits slightly behind Lynch on the set of *The Return*.
Photo courtesy of Showtime/CBS

me to sit next to him and not feel like I was going to curtail him. So maybe it is trust? Or was it just me being cautious? Even still, I would sit behind him because I would never assume. I'm not that kind of producer—that ballsy person. I'm much more conservative and worried to make sure that his experience is good.

Ryan: Would you now have a better way of telling him that the production couldn't afford something he wanted?

Sutherland: For sure. I would say, "You want a crane for this. I understand. If we have to have it, fine. Let's figure out a way to afford that and maybe bring money from something else that we don't need."

Ryan: We have to be sure we talk about the soundtrack from the movie.

Sutherland: It's a great soundtrack. I wasn't involved in that portion at all. I love the David Bowie song. David Lynch told me that when he told David Bowie he wanted to use "I'm Deranged," Bowie said that is his favorite song on the album, but that it was not a popular song.

Ryan: Were you sick of hearing the Rammstein song on set?

Sutherland: David was playing it all the time. Everybody knew that song. We heard it over and over. Whenever I hear that song, I go right back to nodding my head, and I am doing it right now just thinking about it. Some people on set hated it, and others were excited by it.

Ryan: Angelo Badalamenti's score is very different in *Lost Highway* than *Twin Peaks*.

Sutherland: David and Angelo's work is an interesting collaboration because it is true collaboration. They are true partners on their music together. They call each other brother. They are so close. Each one gives something to the other.

Ryan: Were there any deleted scenes from the film?

Sutherland: There was some prison stuff, but not a lot of it. There was a diner scene. It didn't add anything. One of my jobs was when Fred was on death row and he got taken to the electric chair. We had to show every single step, and David wanted it real. I got a hold of a prison warden who was still doing electrocutions. He walked me through each step. We set it up and filmed it exactly as it is done. But that is not in the film.

Ryan: Where does *Lost Highway* fit in Lynch's legacy?

Sutherland: I would hope it would have a prominent place, but it's always overlooked. It didn't do well at the time. There was no group that wanted to see it, the film company just dropped it, and it went by the wayside. I hope there is a resurgence. It should be a prominent part of his library, just like *Dune* should be a part of it. All of his films have something that you take away from it.

Ryan: Do you think it is overlooked because it isn't explained?

Sutherland: I don't like when people complain "Why isn't there any ending?" Why do you have to have people spoon-feed you? Use your own mind to come to conclusions. Don't you have critical thinking skills? I like thinking about a film later or have questions about it. I don't like seeing a film and never thinking about it again. I don't know that there is an absolute interpretation for *Lost Highway*. There are things that are logical and things that are illogical, but if you are thinking about it and you come up with *any* conclusion—that conclusion is what the film is supposed to be—even if it is conflicting. It's like the end of *Gone with the Wind*; that writer was hounded all the time about what happened the next day. Let your mind wander.

CHAPTER 7
DEBBIE ZOLLER

Makeup artist Debbie Zoller spent three years covering Data in metallic makeup and crafting Worf's head on *Star Trek: The Next Generation*. She gave Don Draper that dapper look on *Mad Men*, and made Bill look mean enough to murder in *Kill Bill*. Let's never forget her herculean task of creating Senorita Dido, the Woodsmen, and Mr. C in *Twin Peaks: The Return*. In every project of mine, there is that one interview that takes me by surprise. Debbie Zoller is that interview. It wasn't that I didn't know about her stellar career. It wasn't that I didn't know that her work in *Lost Highway* is amazing. I just wasn't sure that she would be able to remember all the things I wanted to know about how she created the looks of Patricia Arquette's Renee and Alice. Maybe it was that I had such high hopes for finding out what went into creating those looks. She remembered all of it and then some. Debbie Zoller more than met my expectations. To conduct this interview, I sent her screen captures of her work from the film, and I have printed them on the page for readers as we discuss each topic. When I am interviewing someone, I try to focus every bit of my heart and soul on the answers and try to get to the truth as best as I can. In doing so, I tend to get emotionally invested in their life journey. I teared up several times while listening to her stories. Not that they are especially dramatic; it's just how I feel when I talk with someone who is spectacularly skilled at their craft. I will admit, not that anyone asked, I am so passionately sick of mediocrity. So I tend to get overly thrilled when I speak with a master craftsperson. To interact with a professional is always a high for me. Debbie Zoller is an inspiration in how she has managed her path, taken risks, and always succeeded. She had been nominated for ten Emmys and lost them all (including a nomination for her work in *The Return*—voters must have skipped Part 8). Finally, in 2019, she won for *Fosse/Verdon*. I think she is going to win you over more quickly.

Scott Ryan: Have you been able to see the new 4K version of *Lost Highway*?

Debbie Zoller: I went to see it in the theater. I was very nervous. I thought, "What is this going to look like in 4K?" Because it wasn't shot that way. But I thought it looked even more beautiful. I went by myself. I didn't want to go with anybody. I just wanted to be in my

Debbie Zoller stands alongside Amy Shiels, Michael Horse, Sabrina S. Sutherland, Sean Bolger, and Jake Wardle in the glass box at the *Twin Peaks* UK Festival. Photo by Scott Ryan

own thoughts. There was a bigger audience there than I ever expected. I kept moving seats because people would sit next to me, and I would get annoyed. People were probably looking at me like I was a crazy lady. I didn't get any popcorn. I just wanted to be fully present. When it started, I just broke out in a huge grin. It was like going down memory lane for me, remembering how much this film changed me as a makeup artist because David challenges you in every way, because he is an artist himself.

Ryan: Do you think perceptions have changed about the film this time around?

Zoller: When the movie first came out, people were trying to overanalyze it. I have such a unique relationship with David. I don't ask him to explain himself. That was my biggest takeaway from working with him. When the movie came out, David said, "Don't ask me to explain this to you. You have to be intuitive enough to watch the movie and take away from it what you think." It's what your experience is up to the time when you watch this movie, then your brain takes what it wants. That was the problem. People were so excited for this film, then they said, "I don't get it." Well, just sit with it for a minute, and sit in quietness, and you'll get it. You will take away what you need to take away.

Ryan: Right now, we blame everyone's short attention span on our phones. Maybe we were always that way, because there were no phones in 1997 to distract us.

Zoller: We are starting to get lazy. David is not going to give you that classic storybook ending . . . ever. His fans have matured over the years and are now going back and watching *Lost Highway*. Another thing that came back to me was how protective I was of Patricia Arquette and her characters. Almost like a mother bird wrapping her wings around her baby because I could feel Patricia's vulnerabilities. That feeling came back to me when I was sitting there.

Ryan: Patricia talked in interviews about crying in between takes. What pressure does that add to you, as the makeup artist, since you have to make her look strong and powerful?

Zoller: Patricia is my hero. There is nothing that woman cannot do. I learned so much from her about what she brings to the art of acting. There is nothing I wouldn't do for her. There was a moment when she had to cry, and she couldn't cry. She was so dehydrated from all the crying she had done. The *one* time she couldn't cry, I had to bring a bag of chopped up onions and bring them to her so she could shove her face in them and get her tears moving. She can normally cry at the drop of a hat, but because she had been crying for so much over the course of the film, she was like, "I'm done." In makeup, we have a tear blower that has menthol chips in it, and you can blow it in their eye, and it makes them tear up, but even that wasn't working. It's my job, when she comes into the makeup trailer, to get her into her character, whichever one that was, to get her ready. My approach to doing that was that one character was more somber and the other was livelier, so the music we played in the trailer would be different. David was very specific in his music choices. In different scenes, he would have the sound mixer with a speaker, and he would play music which was the beat of the scene. I had never experienced that before. It really changes you in how you approach a scene. When we first started *The Return*, I asked him if he was going to do that again because it helps us as crew members. He said, "Debbie, I am doing that in my own head this time." He had headphones and he had music playing, but just for him.

Ryan: After this film, you worked with Patricia Arquette a lot.

Zoller: I was with her for ten years after that. I got a call from Naomi Watts to do *The Ring Two*. Then I got a call from Patricia saying she got the television series *Medium* and asked if I was available. I couldn't. I suggested Amanda Carroll, and she's still with her.

Ryan: Looking back, you could have been on *Medium* for seven years, but you've done so many other things. Do you feel that was a crossroads for you?

Zoller: When I was on *Star Trek: The Next Generation*, I was hired for three days to do cleanup, and I left three years later. I did Seasons 5, 6, and 7. Michael Westmore was my mentor and my boss. There were people that were on that show that never left. That was their whole career. I remember having that thought that this could be my career, but I thought, "What else is out there?" It was the hardest decision for me to tell Michael that I have to go and see what else is out there.

Ryan: And that led you to David Lynch. What have you learned in working with him?

Zoller: You have to understand how David works. If your ego is bigger than his, you won't last. I really listen to what he says. You have to hear what he wants and then interpret that with such specificity. Learning TM also brings me a better connection as an artist as well.

Ryan: I sent you some pictures, and I thought we would go through them. Let's start with Andy (Michael Massee) and his head on the table. Did you have to do the blood for this?

Zoller: We all worked on this. We put Michael Massee up against the table. I would do the blood, or I'd say, "David, would you like the honor?" I would bring different tools and elements that he can design with. He loves painting, so he uses blood and other food products like paint. Michael's mustache was completely handlaid every day. We didn't have a mustache for him because it was a last-minute additive.

Ryan: What does handlaid mean?

Zoller: We don't draw it. It is actual yak hair that is glued onto his face. We did that every morning. I didn't have one made. Usually, we have ones that are lace backed, and there is a very fine lace, and the hair is attached hair by hair like a wig. I didn't have one of those. This was twenty-five years ago. Now I have a huge stock of things. David said, "I'd like to have a mustache on him," so I hand laid it, meaning you take hair by hair and you glue it, tape it, and trim it. That mustache tells the story of who that character is without you even knowing. That is the point of makeup—period. We assist in storytelling through the art of makeup. That is what we do.

Ryan: I know makeup is important in every film, but there is something about this film. It is ticked up a level in several of the characters. I just love this makeup on Alice. I love the eyeshadow.

Zoller: It's a white eyeshadow, frosty. When I first got the call from Deepak to interview for the job, I didn't even know it was a David Lynch movie. I met with Patty Norris, the production and costume designer. It was Patty who hired me. I went to her office, and she had all of these pictures behind her on a board with color palettes and tones of different scenes. I hadn't even read a script yet, but I asked her questions about the photos. I asked, "Does somebody play two characters in this movie? I can see the difference in the color palettes and the tones." I guess it was that conversation that got me the job, because Patty went to Deepak and said, "She gets it." Based on those designs, before I had ever talked to David, I had this image in my head of the light and the dark between the two characters. Not that Renee is evil, but it is the contrast of the light and the dark.

Ryan: Do you get to see the dresses she will be wearing weeks before so you can plan on all this?

Zoller: Not weeks before. Once Patty had fittings and David approved, I would go to Patty and ask what Patricia would be wearing for each scene. Patricia was so open that she never questioned my choices. She was a blank canvas. She had so much trust in us that she let us do what we felt was right. When you have that kind of trust with an actress, it's a beautiful thing. The character has to fit into David's walls. Every job I do with David, I look at the production design first so I know what walls the actors walk in front of. Then I look at the costumes. I look at the paint colors. I look at the curtains. I look at everything, because it is my job to fit that actor into those decisions.

Ryan: That is because he doesn't make movies; he makes paintings.

Zoller: That is very true. I have to figure out how to work in this scene with the production design and the hair. Because the hair is the frame to the painting.

Ryan: Do you have anything to do with the hair?

Zoller: I try not to because that is not my job description. We have separate categories in our union, so I am only allowed to do makeup, but we have to work together closely. You have to have some kind of input, but you just have to be careful not to step over a line. The hair also goes with the skin tone. If the actress has a certain skin tone and they put a wig on her that is ashy or too yellow, it changes the skin tones. You have to take those things into consideration as well.

Ryan: One more thing on this frame—the lipstick. Is it red and then you put white on top of it or is that a light reflecting?

Zoller: It's a light that is reflecting, but it is also a peachier color, and then I took the white frost from her eyeshadow and put it on her lower lip as a highlight. That way it all coordinates together. She is a beautiful girl. It's all about Alice's reveal.

Ryan: So this is Renee's nail polish. We see it when she pats Fred on his back. What color is that?

Zoller: This is vamp. It is a color by Chanel that was very popular. It became popular when my friend Michelle Bühler used it on Uma Thurman in *Pulp Fiction*.

Ryan: Why does Renee have that color?

Zoller: This is a deep one. I didn't want her to look goth. I didn't want her to look period. I didn't want her to be pigeonholed into any specific look. You draw an idea of a Bettie Page because of the bangs of her hair. When you wear dark nail polish as a woman, you can't see through to her skin. It's not sheer. You can't see the health of a woman. If you have ever had a stress test and they put that clip on your finger to take your blood pressure, you can't do that with dark nail polish on. If you go to a hospital, they have to take dark nail polish off to put that clip on your finger. So this is how my brain works. I wanted Renee to have that dark nail polish so you couldn't see through to her being, her soul, and her health. I wanted her to have dark nail polish, but not black, because black sends a different message.

Ryan: So on this one, is Sheila [Natasha Gregson Wagner] wearing the same color nail polish as Renee?

Zoller: No. Natasha's is metallic gray. I would never use the same color on different actors in the same movie. That will NEVER happen. Each character is unique. This color came about because of what Patty [Norris] dressed her in. Everything in David's movies has a purpose, so her hands are framing Balthy's face. So it is very important that whatever color I choose, it has to work within the confines of what they are wearing. I don't want it to be distracting to the scene, but I want it to make sense. Because Balthy had that leather jacket, and what their color palette was, that is how I chose that nail polish.

Ryan: You spent so much time developing Alice and Renee, but you also have to do that with Sheila. Is it hard to develop Sheila when she is just the girl next door?

Zoller: It's not that you don't put as much effort into Sheila as you do the other characters. Of course you do. It's a specific thought process. It's dealing with the production design, wardrobe, and then I fill in the blanks. With Natasha, she is so beautiful. She doesn't need a lot of makeup. But I wanted her to be really natural because I wanted her to have a completely different vibe than Alice. You could see she is so in love with Balthy, and he likes her, but you can tell there isn't that passion coming from him. You see his entire body come alive when he sees Alice. Balthy thinks Sheila is his girl for right now. She loves him, and then when he sees Alice, an obsession takes over, which is a completely different kind of love.

Ryan: Here we have another nail color.

Zoller: These nails are turquoise green. This polish was from a company called Hard Candy, and it doesn't exist anymore. They were very big in the nineties. I remember telling Patty that I wanted to use this color because it sets off her blond hair, so I asked if I could find a place to use this color. Because Alice smokes cigarettes—it's like *Mad Men,* where you always see their hands—so I wanted her nails to be done because that character would do that.

Ryan: Patricia Arquette said that sometimes she had to get her nails done like four times in a day. Would that have been you that had to do that?

Zoller reunites with her chair and Lynch on the set of *The Return*.
Photo courtesy of Debbie Zoller

Zoller: That's me. We are a one-stop shop. [Laughs.] The nails were such a focus on Patricia. I am digressing for a moment. I had this wooden, old chair that had two arms that folded out with a padded seat and back. That was my makeup chair. David loved that chair. Deepak came up to me and said, "I'll give you fifty bucks for that chair. David wants that chair." I said, "Are you kidding me, Deepak? It cost me two hundred dollars." Deepak said, "I'll give you fifty for it." I said, "Don't give me anything. Let him have it." So I gave David the chair, and I just used a normal director's chair. To this day, he still has this chair. He has added a few accoutrements to the chair; he drilled a cigarette holder and ashtray into it, a cup holder for his coffee. He has really reworked it to make it his own. One of the most beautiful things is knowing he still has it to this day. But during *Lost Highway*, because I was doing Patricia's nails so much, David said he wanted his nails done. So there was a day we were outside filming somewhere and I am out there giving David a manicure. Someone has that picture somewhere. I don't have it. He is sitting in my chair in his khaki pants with a white shirt and his hat on, and I am sitting on an apple box filing and buffing his nails.

Ryan: Next we have the welt on Pete's head.

Zoller: Balthy was twenty when we filmed this. He wasn't legal. We had gone to a place outside Vegas, and he wasn't allowed to gamble. He was the sweetest thing ever. He would sit in my makeup chair, and when I finished with him, he would wink at me as a thank you, and it would melt my heart. He still did that wink when we did *Twin Peaks: The Return*. Michael Burnett was hired to do the effects makeup. I was hired to do the beauty makeup. What David realized was that I was also an effects makeup artist. There were many times when Michael's team would put something on Balthy, and then I would doctor it if David asked me to change things. Like maybe David would want the bump on the other side, or maybe it was too big for this scene, so I would have to remove it and put a bruise on his forehead. Michael and I kind of overlapped when it came to Balthazar and Bill Pullman. If he was in full prosthetics, they would cover that because I was busy with everybody else.

Ryan: You are bound to give him a Klingon forehead if they leave it up to you.

Zoller: Don't laugh, I have one in my stock that Michael Westmore gave me.

Ryan: Anything to add about Bill Pullman's makeup or was that just pretty straightforward?

Zoller: Nothing is ever straightforward with David. Bill would have this scruffy beard throughout the film. He was actually clean-shaven, and I would have to add that depending on where David wanted the scruff. Like in the poster when you see Bill in the car, that is a fake beard that I applied. It kind of shows the demise and arc of his character. The film was shot out of order, so I would have to put that beard on and then take it off, kind of like Patricia's nail polish.

Ryan: Hmm. To be honest, I didn't even notice his scruff.

Zoller: Good. That is the thing. You don't want makeup to pull you out of the film. If it looks fake, then I haven't done my job.

Ryan: You have a flashback scene with different makeup for Alice when she sees Mr. Eddy and has the gun to her head.

Zoller: That is exactly how Patricia felt that day, like she had a gun to her head. She was supposed to be younger. We showed that with her hair and less makeup. We wanted her to look more naive.

Ryan: In the 4K restoration, her lipstick knocked my head backwards. Is this the same lipstick just not with the white eyeshadow highlights?

Zoller: I wanted her to have that red lipstick because she is a powerful woman in a powerless situation. Red lipstick signifies that. Red lipstick for a woman is a power color. It looks like the 4K may have altered the tone a bit because I don't remember it being that orange, but it was definitely in the red family. Her eyes were so striking, and I wanted her makeup to be completely different from what Alice is now. We edged her up a bit so you could see the evolution of who she became when she went to work for Mr. Eddy.

Ryan: She is scared at first, but she loses that as she approaches Mr. Eddy and gains the power back. That had to be hard for her to do that day, and hard for you as well.

Zoller: Yeah. The whole point of my job is to make the actress feel comfortable in whatever scene she is about to approach, but also knowing when not to get involved. You have to allow them their process. You can't smother them, and you can't ignore them. There is a fine line of social cues that you have to learn in this business. Now I

have conversations with the actors and ask them about their process. I had to have that conversation with Sam Rockwell on *Fosse/Verdon*. He didn't like to be fussed over. But we had so many things we had to do with that character, so we came up with a safe word for when I should leave him alone when he is preparing. Patricia never had that with me. She always allowed me to approach her. David wouldn't want anyone to disturb a scene. Noah Baumbach and Steven Spielberg are the same way.

Ryan: Here we have Patricia Arquette in that amazing dress. Did you feel pressure that you are doing a scene where she has to be so beautiful or it won't serve the plot?

Zoller: I think it depends on how prepared you are. I knew exactly what I wanted to do with this character. The pressure is the reveal when she walks on set and looking at David's face. That says it all. So I know when he is happy, and when he is questioning a choice. At that time, this was my first job with David. There might have been more pressure in that respect because I wanted to please him. I am not asking him to explain himself. I am listening to what he is telling me, and then I bring what I think is correct to the scene. He wants you to think, and that is the beauty of working with him as an artist. He does allow you to bring your ideas to the table as long as you listen to what he is asking for. Patricia brought so much to this character, and then Patty Norris knew how to fit a dress to her body. Patricia's body is so beautiful in this dress. I love the length, the color, how it clings to her, and how the wig extends that color to the dress. It all goes together. She has white nails here. It is making her look ethereal and angelic.

Ryan: Tell me about the sandstorm in the desert and how that affected your job.

Zoller: Balthy and Patricia both got a salt scrub because that wind was so intense. We all were eating sand for days. They would bring them to a tent, and I would brush them off with a big makeup brush so they didn't look like they had powder all over them. When they were laying in the sand, I just left them alone. Patricia is so good how she can bring elements into her acting that she is actually fixing something. She would touch Balthy in such a way that if she saw there was sand stuck to his face, she would remove it. That is how brilliant she is.

Ryan: According to the script, Renee is supposed to be eight years older than Alice. Did you age her either way?

Zoller: That was not up to me. That is done through Patricia's acting, with the giggling she does as Alice, or the sweetness. Renee's look came about because we wanted her to look more mature and more polished. Based on the production design and the black robe that she wears in the house, it all had to go together where she is very put together but not with a tremendous amount of effort.

Ryan: What kind of eyeshadow does she have?

Zoller: This is all in the neutral tones. The lipstick is vamp as well to match the nails. I wanted her eyes to be more sultry and more doe shaped which is a rounder shape. The only thing I wanted Alice and Renee to have in common is the eyebrows, so I didn't change the shape between the two characters. That is the one thing that connects them.

Ryan: With Renee, it sometimes looks like she is a redhead and sometimes brunette.

Zoller: There was a scene in the bathroom and it's all red in *Lost Highway*. I didn't know that at the last minute, David changed the lighting to make it all red. It was almost like a darkroom. Lighting changes makeup, so I will always talk to the director and the DP to ask if there is specific lighting, so that my choices make sense. When you put makeup in front of red, everything turns black.

Ryan: So we finally get to the Mystery Man.

Zoller: I had met Robert Blake when I was in college. He came to speak at UCLA, and I worked in student government and was assigned to him to be his greeter. Years later, we are in the desert shooting *Lost Highway*. Those were the first scenes he shot on the film, and I hadn't worked with him yet. I had a friend in college that was a big jokester, and he would call me and pretend to be celebrities. I am in my hotel, and I get a call. "Debbie, this is Robert Blake, I want to talk to you about my makeup." I am thinking it is my friend Donnie. He asks me, "What can we do to make my look be different?" I said, "Why don't we just shave your eyebrows?" He said, "Well, if you think that would go with the character." Then I realized I am *actually* talking to Robert Blake. I almost fainted. I had to tell him the story, and he burst out in that weird, crazy laugh that he has in the movie. We did a makeup test, and David wanted him really pale, and sure enough, we shaved his eyebrows.

Ryan: That is so crazy that it was just a joke, but it makes him so creepy.

Zoller: David also wanted his ears to stick out. We were way out in the desert, and I didn't have any tools to do that. I called one of my makeup artist friends, and they suggested I use chewing gum because that is what they did in *Gandhi*. I had mortician's wax. I built up the back of his ears with spirit gum and cotton, and then I sculpted mortician's wax over it and pushed his ears out. I warned David that I would get it as smooth as I could in the back but to be careful doing over-the-shoulder shots. It looked fine and nobody ever noticed—even on the 4K it looks good. We framed his eyes with brown eyeshadow; his lips look a little bit too toned, but that is probably the 4K alteration.

Ryan: I noticed in the 4K that he isn't all white. It's kind of skin and kind of white. It looked all white on VHS, but now, it's not like he is in a Tim Burton movie.

Zoller: Right. It is a pale tone; it isn't white. David wanted him to look otherworldly, but we didn't want you to know if he was alive or dead, or from this realm, or if he is in Bill's imagination. That is why he is the Mystery Man, because you don't know how or where he comes from.

Ryan: I love that it was your idea to shave his eyebrows.

Zoller: It was just a mortifying joke.

CHAPTER 8
THE SOUNDTRACK

There is no way to analyze a Lynch film and not spend a good portion of the research on the music. Whether you take the score that plays under the scenes, the songs that come from inside the scenes or plays on top of them, or if you look at the soundscape that rumbles through all of Lynch's work, you simply cannot ignore the sounds of a Lynch film. It all started with *Eraserhead,* which has a continuous sound of throbbing dread. A sound that doesn't always logically match the action of the scenes. I have watched *Eraserhead* with the subtitles on and the volume almost completely turned off. It was that viewing that allowed me to understand the plot and not be distracted by the noise. In watching Lynch's short films back-to-back, I noticed how often he creates a soundscape that launches an assault on the viewer. It is almost like he is begging the viewer to wince in pain while watching his characters live out their lives.

Twin Peaks had wall-to-wall music and that music is possibly the only reliable narrator in the entire story. *The Straight Story* had Angelo Badalamenti channeling his inner Midwest-folk-country feel. With *Lost Highway*, it almost seems as if Lynch foresaw how the future music culture would soon consume music by creating the ultimate mixtape for mid-nineties alternative music that predated Spotify or iPods by decades. Soon those devices would have listeners streaming playlists and jumping from one artist to another. The *Lost Highway* soundtrack does it for the listener.

Along with this playlist, *Lost Highway* has the typical Lynchian uneasy sound rumblings to make the hallways seem eerier, the out-of-focus moments more unsettling, and the humming of empty rooms more ominous. The reason the viewer suspects that violence is lurking in the Madison house doesn't come from the set. The set is beautiful. The Madisons seem like a financially well-off couple. Renee is uncommonly beautiful, Fred is a working musician, but despite everything on the surface looking wonderful, there is that constant rumble to let viewers know something is wrong. What else could that rumble represent? It lets viewers know that nothing but trouble awaits once the first videotape is left on the doorstep. It makes that dark hallway feel like evil will be found at the end of it. Unease is everywhere in the house. Those sounds were created by a superstar of the alternative music scene: the lead singer of Nine Inch Nails, Trent Reznor, who also produced the soundtrack album.

Over the following pages, I describe each track on the soundtrack, where it played in the film, and try to give a little history of the song. This was my favorite part of writing this book. To get to listen to this music, find where it played in the film, and do research on where the song originated from, honestly gave me the most insight into what *Lost Highway* is really about. The music or sound design is where the truth always lies. Because Lynch layers ambient noise, rumbles, sound effects, and dialogue, and then places music on top of all that, several of these tracks could be hidden in other scenes in addition to where I mention them, but I tried to find the most prominent scene. As always, I suggest that you listen to each track as you read. Let's *alternatively* rock.

"I'm Deranged" (edit) – David Bowie – 2:37
This David Bowie track begins the movie and the soundtrack. It also ends both items. There are subtle differences between the versions. The opener has an introduction where the reprise starts with an a capella vocal. At least there are differences between the two. I've never understood why my 1978 *Grease* album had the theme song on the album two times. Did we really need to be told, "Grease is the word," twice? (Answer: hells yeah.) It isn't a new thing for a soundtrack to

open and close with the same song, but I think this is more than just rounding out the soundtrack. I believe the reason both the soundtrack and movie open and close with "I'm Deranged" is because the entire movie *is the song*. That is the only part of the film we can trust. That's all it was—a police car chase where Fred listens to this song. So even the soundtrack is a psychogenic fugue. Within Fred's diluted fantasy, he has an entire car mixtape, CD, or playlist (depending on your age) that scores his attempted escape from the police. We know from the sound at the beginning of the movie of the curtains opening, which sounds a lot like prison bars, that Fred is apprehended. That opening shot of him in his house could easily be Fred smoking a cigarette on a jail bunk bed. In the film, viewers watch his fantasy in between the time they hear the song. On the record, listeners hear his fantasy playlist when they listen to the soundtrack. "Cruise me, Baby," David Bowie sings in the chorus. Whether that is a police cruiser, cruise control, or cruising around town is up to you. Fred goes through his fantasy of a film and a soundtrack.

"Videodrones; Questions" – Trent Reznor featuring Peter Christopherson – 0:44
This track is the "music" that plays when Fred and Renee watch the videotapes that are dropped off at their house by an unseen person. However, for the soundtrack, the dialogue that is heard during this track is lifted from the sex scene with Fred and Renee. Fred is heard struggling to achieve climax, and then Renee says, "It's OK. It's OK." Why Trent Reznor decided to mix these different elements from two scenes together is unclear. The music that scores the sex scene is actually a Badalamenti piece.

Reznor explained how he created this sound to *Pitchfork* in 2016: "I had a white noise generator that became pretty musical when you tuned it; you normally used to tune rooms, but it had a pitch in it and it was weirdly soothing." He thinks this noise is soothing? Makes you wonder what else soothes him. A dentist's drill? James Hurley's singing?

Peter Christopherson is credited as cocreating the track and is a member of the band Coil. (Not to be confused with the band This

Mortal Coil, which we will discuss later and is a completely different musical act.) Coil worked with Nine Inch Nails on several remixes. According to the other member of Coil, John Balance, Reznor wanted to use a Coil song on the soundtrack, but Lynch declined. Balance told Jon Whitney in a 1997 interview for Brainwashed.com, "You know, with *Lost Highway*, Trent literally forced down David Lynch's throat saying 'Look, please put this Coil stuff on.' You know he really did help to get us on that soundtrack but he [Lynch] wasn't interested. He wanted David Bowie, he wanted Marilyn Manson, he wanted whoever he could get. He just said, 'These people are really big. I want this film to be really big.' He didn't give a fuck about the integrity." It does seem like the band got something in the movie, if not the soundtrack, as in another interview Balance did mention that they do get residuals from the film, but maybe that is this track.

"The Perfect Drug" – Nine Inch Nails – 5:42

This track starts immediately as if the prior track is the intro to "The Perfect Drug." Trent Reznor doesn't seem to be a fan of his own track. In some ways, I don't blame him. He mentioned to *Rolling Stone* in 1997 that he was creating the album for "the person who hates pop music who buys this David Lynch soundtrack, they will get what they want out of it." But I would submit that the chorus of "The Perfect Drug" is pretty darn poppy. It is very singable and repeats the same line over and over, "You are the perfect drug." I find this earworm stuck in my head like plenty of awful pop songs that played on the radio back when there was radio. Reznor said in 2016 to *Pitchfork*, "A few years after *Lost Highway* I finally got my shit together and got sober. When I think back, that was one of my regrets—I wasn't at 100 percent during the time I spent with [Lynch] on *Lost Highway*. I was struggling to keep my shit together, convincing myself that it was business as usual. Looking back I know that I could have been better." He also mentioned on the BBC in 2005 that this song wouldn't be in his top hundred songs. That being said, it charted as high as number eleven on *Billboard's* Alternative Airplay chart in 1997 and was the second single released from the soundtrack.

This song isn't really in the movie. There is a bit of the drum solo during the scene where Mr. Eddy is chasing the tailgater, but that is about it. There is so much noise in the scene that it is hard to find, but like a few of the other songs on this soundtrack, it's just a portion and it's buried under the soundscapes that Lynch created.

"Red Bats with Teeth" – Angelo Badalamenti – 2:57
Here is the song that made me eject that VHS all those years ago. Listening to the full track today, the first two minutes really aren't that far off from a *Twin Peaks* saxophone/jazz number. I definitely overreacted to it the first time I heard the song. It's the last minute where things go a little nuts. David Lynch said in *Pretty as a Picture*, "Fred Madison plays the sax but it's more the solo that is the real important thing. It's just got to be insane." In the same documentary, Bill Pullman said, "I don't have to play it; all I have to do is sell it. This is *show* business. This is not *accuracy* business. I've got the experience that David created with the music. It starts somewhat melodic, then goes berserk. It goes fierce; it goes reptilian brain." No way I can describe this song better than that.

"Haunting & Heartbreaking" – Angelo Badalamenti – 2:09
This Badalamenti track sounds like the composer we know and love. This track could have easily fit in *Twin Peaks: The Return*. In fact, there is a song in *The Return* called "Heartbreaking." Given the many anecdotes of Lynch sitting side by side with Badalamenti and giving him direction for their songs, I am sure heartbreaking is a term Lynch uses to describe characters, plots, or emotions he is creating. For this film, it is Sheila whose heart is breaking. This track scores the scene on the front lawn as Sheila breaks up with Pete when she realizes that Pete no longer cares for her. I wish the name of this song was "Sheila's Theme," as it's hard to hear the track and not think of Natasha Gregson Wagner's expressive face. This song has the synth sound and dimensioned chords that are associated with *Fire Walk With Me, Twin Peaks,* and *Mulholland Dr.*. I always wonder what alternative rock music fans who bought the album to listen to the rock stars of the nineties thought of this track. I like to think it led them to purchase many other Badalamenti albums.

"Eye" – The Smashing Pumpkins – 4:51
This song reached number eight on *Billboard*'s Alternative Airplay chart in 1997 and was the first single off the album. Lynch used the song in the nightclub scene where Sheila and Pete dance and reunite after his release from prison. According to the Smashing Pumpkins Recording Sessions Wiki, the track was an instrumental written for Shaquille O'Neal to rap over. He passed on it, and it ended up in the new Lynch project. Oh, the nineties, was there nothing that you couldn't do?

"Dub Driving" – Angelo Badalamenti – 3:43
I would consider this the main theme for the film. This original Badalamenti instrumental expertly captures the feel of the film. The song is used to score Sheila and Pete's love scene in the car. The track has shades of "The Pink Room" from *Fire Walk With Me*. Not that they sound the same, but the track is built with the same concept. The bass keeps playing the same refrain over and over again. On top of the sexy, dark, and murky beat is an electric guitar that plays chords and gives that circling feeling of being in a loop of a sexually charged moment of rock 'n' roll, sex, and drugs. It embodies the feeling of the Pete section of the film in under four minutes. Bravo, Angelo.

"Mr. Eddy's Theme 1" – Barry Adamson – 3:31
This song has a quote from Robert Loggia that can immediately bring a smile to my face. I do love that this soundtrack uses dialogue from the movie. While many soundtracks did this back in the sixties and seventies, it was Quentin Tarantino who brought the idea back into vogue with *Reservoir Dogs* and *Pulp Fiction*. "Theme 1" plays at the beginning of Pete's ride with Mr. Eddy to check out the noise that Mr. Eddy's car is making. "Theme 2" kicks in when the tailgater starts getting a touch too close to the car. This has a similar bass feel to "Dub Driving" but isn't quite as sexy. But then again, not sure Mr. Eddy is quite as appealing as Sheila is.

"This Magic Moment" – Lou Reed – 3:23
Lou Reed brings to musical life Pete's fantasy girl. The track kicks

in when he, and viewers, first lay eyes on the blonde bombshell that is Alice. The song sure is an oldie but a goodie. Written by one of the most famous songwriters of the sixties, Doc Pomus, with Mort Shuman, this song was originally recorded by The Drifters. It sets viewers of Lynch's generation back to the sounds of pop sixties music but covered with the darker sound of Lou Reed and the nineties. Lynch singled this track out in his book *Room to Dream,* saying, "Lou Reed's version of 'This Magic Moment' is in the film, too, and it's the all-time best version of that song. I love the drums in that song, and I love the way Lou sings it and it's perfect for that scene." The magic moment is Pete having a love-at-first-sight moment with the Marilyn Monroe version of Alice. Slow motion is used to extend the moment for Pete, as we all know he is going to get in a lot of trouble because of this girl. It is by design that this song plays *after* we have already seen Mr. Eddy beat a guy to a pulp just for tailgating. We don't have to imagine what Mr. Eddy would do to any guy who tries to tailgate his girl.

"Mr. Eddy's Theme 2" – Barry Adamson – 2:13
This song is "smooth as shit from a duck's ass," as Mr. Eddy might say. This has the feel of a song that could have been Badalamenti, but isn't. Barry Adamson is a UK rocker who has worked with Nick Cave and the Bad Seeds, as well as others. This song plays in probably what was the most famous scene in the movie, the tailgating scene. I suggest you do not listen to this track in your car if you are experiencing road rage. But seriously, wouldn't Mr. Eddy make the best Uber driver ever?

"Fred & Renee Make Love" – Angelo Badalamenti – 2:04
This instrumental track plays, albeit briefly, in the scene where Fred and Renee attempt to have sex. I am thinking Angelo wanted to give Fred some dignity when he named this track, so he didn't call it "Fred & Renee Try to Make Love And Then Sit In Awkward Silence While Fred Tells Her He Mistakenly Masturbated Moments Before She Came to Bed." This is another track where Reznor, who is the executive producer on this album, not Lynch, used dialogue that doesn't go with this track. He has Pete saying, "I want you." Pete says

this toward the end of the film when Alice and Pete have sex in the car headlights in the middle of desert. The song that plays during Alice and Pete's sex scene is "Song to the Siren" by This Mortal Coil. This song also plays for a moment in the scene where Fred and Alice attempt their lovemaking. So just like with *Fire Walk With Me*, the reliable narrator is the sound. The fact that "Song to the Siren" plays in both scenes, added in with the fact that the dialogue is shuffled around on the soundtrack, gives us a very big clue that Fred was *not* a successful lover and doesn't satisfy Renee, but in his fantasy as Pete, he has sex outdoors in a sandstorm in a spotlight. "Siren" plays for a brief moment one other time, when Fred is in jail and he sees the cabin exploding in his mind. This makes sense, as this is the location of his manly sex on the beach. "Siren" is a thread between the sex he had with Renee and the sex he wishes he had with her. That track is not on the album. The band wouldn't give the rights for that. It's a shame, as it's such an important song to the film.

"Apple of Sodom" – Marilyn Manson – 4:26
For a book that started off with a quote from Broadway legend Stephen Sondheim, it will come to no one's surprise that Marilyn Manson's music doesn't jive with my sensibility. This song plays in the scene where Pete sits in his room, sees spiders and bugs around the room, and he sees just the head of Alice floating in the dark. The camera blurs in and out until Pete leaves on his motorcycle to see Alice. You really can't hear the voice of Marilyn Manson in the film. The song certainly fits the scene and gives the desired mood. In doing research on the song, Manson mentions this song was partially inspired by his "love" for Fiona Apple. He then goes on to say the most disgusting things about her, which would certainly counteract any true love for an artist, especially someone as sensitive and talented as Fiona Apple. There are con artist/provocateurs a plenty in every decade of American culture. This Joke-Jack was just one of them from the nineties. Manson always got press by saying horrible things, and I don't believe this song had anything to do with Fiona Apple. He was just trying to feed off her popularity, which was at its height at that point in time. I think the one good thing about putting a camera on everyone's phone in

our current decade is that it makes it a lot harder to shock the media into making a person famous for saying and doing disgusting things because everyone can do it, and besides a Kardashian or two, most of them come and go pretty quickly. Manson's involvement with controversial activities has removed him from public life at this point, but America loves a second act. Who knows what his future will entail, but just like with O. J., I won't be consuming any of it.

"Insensatez" – Antônio Carlos Jobim – 2:53
From one type of music to the other: this track has that Sunday morning coffee feeling that I love. It might be my favorite instrumental track on the album. This plays when Pete is released from jail in a scene that almost looks like it could have been cut from *Blue Velvet*. Pete is just hanging around in a hammock, sitting in the backyard, looking at green grass, wearing a red shirt, and staring over the fence at a blue kiddie pool with a pink ball floating in it. In a film where most of the colors are just different shades of black, this colorful scene, scored with a bossa nova beat, resets the movie and almost behaves like the opening credits to the Pete section of the film.

Interestingly, this song does have lyrics and was recorded by Sting on the 1994 *Red Hot and Rio* compilation. They fit the film. The title translates to "How Insensitive." The singer laments, "Now she's gone away and I'm alone with a memory of her last look." This could have related to Fred having murdered Renee. It would have been great to have the track with lyrics in the film. In hearing the instrumental version that is on the record, one could guess this is an old sixties song, but it was written in the nineties. I love how contemporary the music is for this film. Most of Lynch's other soundtracks hearken back to the feel of the fifties or sixties. This film is set smack-dab in the heart of the nineties.

"Something Wicked This Way Comes" (edit) – Barry Adamson – 2:54
This song plays at the party that Fred and Renee attend, moments before the Mystery Man appears to tell Fred that he is at the party and at Fred's house. One wonders if Lynch picked this track from the name alone, because something wicked is certainly just about to come. The

track is from Adamson's 1996 album. Again, here is a contemporary song that, while it might feel like a track that was from the past, is a current song. The Adamson track came from *Oedipus Schmoedipus*, which was his latest album.

"I Put a Spell on You" – Marilyn Manson – 3:30
Since I am not a fan of Manson, I'll let Lynch talk about him. While answering questions from Davidlynch.com years ago, Lynch said, "He's got his own thing going. He really intuits the songs and has a great musical sense. They stand out. So even if he does a cover it is so him and so great musically." Written by Screamin' Jay Hawkins, "I Put a Spell on You" is a classic fifties song that many people have covered. (My personal favorite is by She & Him.) This cover song plays in the scene where Alice is forced to strip at gunpoint in front of Mr. Eddy and his gang. The uneasy feel that Manson brings to this classic song is perfect for the scene.

The singer exclaims they "put a spell on you because you are mine." This has many connections to the film, not the least of which is when Alice tells Pete that "You'll never have me."

When analyzing any scene in the film, one must always look at every scene from two perspectives. You have the scene as it is presented and then the fact that the entire movie is filtered through a mad man's mind. Taking the strip scene as presented, we have Mr. Eddy, who appears to be in control. He is sitting in a comfy chair while everyone stands around him. He is in charge of the man who holds the gun; he forces Alice to strip and get on her knees in front of him. However, the person that is casting the spell is Alice on Mr. Eddy. He may feel he is in control, but Alice doesn't show a glimmer of fear. She is owning him. He may hold the gun, but it will be her that pulls his trigger. Now, going to the second level of the scene, which means Fred's imagination. He would assume that his wife would only have sex with another man at gunpoint and if a spell was cast on her. She would not be able to have ownership of who she has sex with, but because he despises her, and all women, she doesn't cry; she begins to enjoys it.

"Fats Revisited" – Angelo Badalamenti – 2:31
Here is the Badalamenti we know and love. We have that wandering bass line and a synth sound on top. This certainly has the flavor of "Audrey's Dance" from *Twin Peaks*. One assumes that Fats is a reference to Fats Domino. This track is not used in the film. However, it was used as the end credits to the *Lost Highway* documentary *Pretty as a Picture*. If you haven't seen it, it really is a great documentary. One of the scenes in it is Lynch and Badalamenti working with the City of Prague Philharmonic. Badalamenti recorded "Fred & Renee Make Love," "Haunting and Heartbreaking," and "The Police" with the philharmonic.

The documentary also shows a scene of Natasha Gregson Wagner and another actress dancing at a drive-in restaurant. While they are dancing, we see a speaker is placed at Lynch's feet as he approves their dance. The song that is playing is "Fats Revisited." This scene was cut from the film, and there went the song. Since this is a documentary, it certainly could be that the filmmakers added this song in editing. There would really be no way for me to know for sure, but I am pretty sure it wasn't done in post because there is a speaker in the scene, the song plays only when they show those clips, and it doesn't play when they cut to studio interviews. The actresses seem to be dancing to the beat of this song, and the scene, while in the script, is not in the film. Online, there are plenty of people trying to solve the mystery of where this song is played in the film. I am happy to solve this one mystery.

"Fred's World" – Angelo Badalamenti – 3:01
This has the synth chords and slow movement that score much of *Mulholland Dr.*. This track is a hard one to find in the film. It is played under a lot of noise when Fred transforms into Pete. It is playing when the car is driving, Pete is seen standing off to the side, and Fred has his seizure and becomes Pete. For such a beautiful track, we really don't get to hear much of it in the film. This is the kind of track that might very well be buried in several other scenes, as it is such a mood setter, and Lynch might be using it to layer several scenes with Fred. As we all know, the key to *Lost Highway* is remembering that everything you see is Fred's world.

"Rammstein" (edit) – Rammstein – 3:26

By far the song that almost every cast and crew member mentioned in their interviews was this song. "Rammstein" is taken from the album *Herzeleid* which translates to "heartbreak." (There's that word again.) It is just an unrelenting piece of music. "Rammstein" is translated to "ramming stone," which is basically what this song does to your eardrums. It just rams it over and over again into your head. As told in many of the interviews in this book, Lynch played this song on set during the scene in the hotel as Fred searches for Dick Laurent and Renee. That entire sequence was designed to be scored with this heavy metal song. The song also plays while Fred kills Dick Laurent.

While this is also not my kind of music, I actually kind of love it. One time my teenage daughter came home from school while this song was playing, and she was quite certain someone had stolen her dad and replaced him with a doppelgänger. Hey, it's a song from a Lynch film; it wasn't a bad guess. This track was released in 1995 and is another example of a song that was used in the film that was from that exact time. I really love how "of its time" the *Lost Highway* soundtrack is.

"Hollywood Sunset" – Barry Adamson – 2:01

The third Barry Adamson song scores the scene directly following "This Magic Moment." Pete tells Alice he can't go out with her, and she starts to call a cab to return home. Pete takes a second look at Alice and her perfect dress, makeup, and smile and does what we all knew he was going to do. He takes off with Alice. Who can blame him? Patricia Arquette looks amazing in this scene. This Adamson track has a sexy bass line that keeps you bobbing your head and sets a perfect tone for the scene. This track is very similar to Badalamenti's "Dub Driving." Both songs are used to score Pete's attraction to either Alice or Sheila.

"Heirate mich" (edit) – Rammstein – 3:02

"Heirate mich" is translated as "Marry Me" and starts to play in the film as soon as Pete enters Andy's house and sees the porno film showing Alice taking it from behind. The juxtaposition of his wanting to run away and marry his love, colliding with the reality of watching her in a porno film while she has sex with Andy upstairs, is right where Pete's mindset is. He sees her stockings, her dress, her purse all laid out on the floor as the deep lead vocal of Till Lindemann speaks/sings the opening lines of the song. Jealousy and rage has now completely overtaken Pete in the way that it did with Fred. The next thing we see Pete do is murder Andy. Fred may have tried to create a new version of himself, but he is once again a murderer.

"Police" – Angelo Badalamenti – 1:40
This short Badalamenti track is basically strings just slowly holding the tension and moving up a step as the song goes on to keep the listener on edge. The track is playing under other songs as Fred tries to escape the police at the end of the movie, before the car chase kicks in. The song on the album ends with the line "Dick Laurent is dead." (How has no one sold a T-shirt with that on it?) In the film, Bill Pullman delivers this line just before the track begins, but on the soundtrack, it ends the song. This is the second time we hear the line in the film. The first time he heard it; the second time he said it. Which is the real one? My guess would be the second one. After he murders Renee, he goes off to kill Dick Laurent. By the time he gets back to his house, he has already purged from his memory that he killed Renee, and so he pushes the button to let her know that he has killed the man he thought she was having an affair with. He is basically telling this to an empty house. The first time we hear "Dick Laurent is dead" in the film—that is all in his imagination.

"Driver Down" – Trent Reznor – 5:18
This is the song that plays over "The Police" as the chase scene begins. Trent Reznor wrote this instrumental piece that scores the final scene before the end credits. It really is a medley of the musical themes used throughout the film. After starting with a hard rock guitar riff, a spastic saxophone solo comes in around three minutes into the track. Around three and a half minutes in, a piano takes the medley with remnants of the title song, "I'm Deranged," which plays next. The hard guitars fade out, leaving just the piano and sax. It leaves a very

unsettled listener with only their thoughts on what happened in the film. The film doesn't use this bare-bones part of the song. In the film, Fred transforms again; and the film goes quiet and then we hear the reprise of …

"I'm Deranged" (reprise) – David Bowie – 3:48
We are back where we started. As pointed out earlier in this chapter, this is a slightly longer version. It has an a capella beginning and runs a minute longer. Just like the film, the entire soundtrack starts and ends with one simple thought: Fred is deranged.

Lost Highway, under the direction of Lynch, Reznor, and Badalamenti is a masterpiece of how to translate a film to a record.

The original album cover art for the soundtrack of Lost Highway.
Photo courtesy of Interscope Records

CHAPTER 9
PETER DEMING

Peter Deming has worked as Lynch's director of photography (DP) for more hours than any other artist. The DP is in charge of photographing exactly what David Lynch is trying to capture on film. Basically, he has to interpret what is going on in Lynch's head and transport it to the silver screen. How would you like to have that job? Interviewing Deming is an exercise in time management. Do I ask him about the black-and-white Part 8 of *Twin Peaks: The Return*? Club Silencio in *Mulholland Dr.*? What about capturing a blackout in *Hotel Room*? He has photographed some of Lynch's most artistic scenes, including my all-time favorite scene, the mauve palace in Part 3. Where does one begin to question someone who has been a part of such amazing art? Well, this is a book about *Lost Highway*, so I had to begin there. But to be fair, even if this was a book about one of those other projects, I would have wanted to get to the bottom of how he lit a hallway in complete and utter blackness and then projected that image onto a lit screen. The definition of oxymoron should be someone whose job it is to light darkness. Peter Deming's specialty is capturing what can't be seen and David Lynch doesn't want to be seen. For this interview, I sent Deming screen captures for us to discuss, as I have done for other interviews. However, this is the only time an interviewee sent *me* back better screen captures to use. He went through his files and gave some beautiful shots from the film. They have been used throughout the book and are used in this interview.

Scott Ryan: Tell me how *Lost Highway* came into your life.

Peter Deming: I'd been working with David for a little while on some short-form stuff and commercials. I had gotten back to Los Angeles around the summer of 1995, David called me, told me he's doing this movie, and asked me if I wanted to shoot it. Of course I said yes.

Ryan: This was your first feature film with him?

Deming: Yes, it was.

Ryan: Any apprehension of making that leap with him?

Deming: No. I'd been shooting features for a while, so I wasn't concerned about doing a movie. Obviously doing a movie with David would be a different singular experience, but there was no apprehension. I said yes immediately.

Ryan: I recently watched *The Godfather* and kept thinking about *Lost Highway* because of all the dark scenes. Did *The Godfather* have any influence on you with all of the extremely dark black colors that you capture in *Lost Highway*?

Deming: No, it didn't really. I think obviously dark is something that David has visually always embraced, so I knew that was coming. To the extent that we went dark on a lot of scenes, that was new for me. We did a little bit of testing, and most of it is trusting your instincts on the day. The most challenging was out in the desert at the cabin and the driving scenes, where there is really no ground light, no practicals; there is nothing.

Ryan: Let's start with the opening credits. You don't get any pixelation or the white poppy stuff that happens when filmmakers try to capture pitch dark. How were you technically able to capture that with the headlights from the car on the bottom of the screen and the blackest black on top?

Deming: Anyone who has exposed film negatives knows that when you have a lot of black in the frame, you have to give whatever highlights or exposed parts a little extra exposure. I'd typically overexpose the highlights a stop or two depending on what they were, so that I could print the film back down to a normal brightness, and then that's when those blacks crush down and become really black, really rich, and you're not able to see into them at all. There were parts of the film where David didn't want that—he wanted more of a murky black, which he found more unsettling and creepy.

Ryan: There is nothing more unsettling than the hallway with Bill Pullman. There are many beautiful shots in *Lost Highway*, but that is extremely unsettling. Talk about filming that scene.

Deming: There is a shot where he comes out of the bedroom and walks away from us down the hallway and disappears into the black—

you don't see which way he goes. This was actually one of the few shots we discussed in prep. It was designed with costumes and set design to aid this effect. Obviously the other component is the lighting and letting the light fall off enough so that he does go into black. So it was a combination of those things and what I just described, giving it an extra exposure so that once you print it down to be normal looking or even darker, the blacks will be so rich that it swallows up anything that doesn't have enough light on it. The day we shot it, I called the lab and had the same discussion with the dailies color timer about what it needed to be for dailies the next day.

Ryan: Was that filmed in the house or did you build this in a soundstage?

Deming: That was in the house. The layout of the house was very specific, so the set people moved a bunch of walls around. Patty Norris, who designed both the costumes and the production, decided that Bill Pullman would be in black. I was hoping that Bill would have a long-sleeve shirt, but he didn't. I was a little concerned about his arms. At the end of the hallway, we basically had black drapery, which is probably the densest black fabric you can imagine—sort of the black version of all the red drapes David uses in *Twin Peaks*. I knew as far as costumes and design that I was in good territory. It was just up to creating the light that would fall off enough so that he wouldn't be lit by the time he had to turn a corner, which thankfully you never notice, since he went dark.

Ryan: The living room with the pastel wall and the light carpet has such interesting colors. You have the lamp in there, so you have to get the lighting right. Tell me about filming in that room in daytime versus nighttime. You never really see a window—was there a window or is that artificial light?

Deming: There is a skylight and two little skinny vertical windows in the room which you see over the course of a few scenes. Then there is the light on the table. For the day scenes, it was sort of a combination of a brackish light—some of it warm, with some of the skylight being cooler during the daytime, since it isn't actual sunlight. The night shots were motivated by the lamp on the table, which David actually made.

Ryan: Deepak talked about how they couldn't find a set so they bought a house and rebuilt it to be what he wanted—is this rare?

Deming: That's the only time it's happened to me. [Laughs.]

Ryan: Let's go to the desert. Discuss the challenges of capturing the cabin, setting it on fire, and what were the conditions like filming there?

Deming: That was out in Death Valley, and it was a little chilly, as I recall. The tough part was that it was super windy and dusty. It's one thing to create wind for a scene and then have the ability to turn it off between takes and setups, but this wasn't the case. On the first night, we shot them arriving and the love scene, and it was just super windy all night long, which slowed down production a little bit. However, when you watch the scene, it adds an amazing mood. The second night, we had a number of shots still outside and an interior shot in the cabin with the Mystery Man. We had to create that wind so we could match the first night. Fortunately there is sort of a natural break going inside the cabin and then out before Bill Pullman's character shows up. Whatever we lacked to make wind was sort of mitigated by the change in scenery a little bit. But if we had to reload the camera, we had to go inside the van—you couldn't be outside for very long.

I remember going back to the hotel when it became morning and trying to clean all of the dust out of all orifices.

Ryan: How about exploding the shed? Did you build that shed to blow it up?

Deming: We built the cabin, and it wasn't the plan to blow it up. On the third night, we shot the Mr. Eddy scene, and while we were packing up, David asked, "What happens to the cabin?" I think initially he was interested in the wood so he could use it in his woodshop. Deepak said, "They'll come and tear it down." David said, "Can't we just blow it up?" We were out in the middle of the desert, it was probably four o'clock in the morning, and we weren't really permitted for that as I recall. We went to Gary D'Amico, who did the special effects, and said, "Gary, can you blow up the cabin?" There's not a special effects person in the industry who wouldn't jump at that chance, so he loaded it up with what he had, and we got three cameras out, and we just blew it up.

Ryan: When you went to work that day, you didn't know you were going to blow up that cabin, and then you blew it up?

Deming: Yes, exactly. You can only admit to doing something like that years later. Given where we were, there was really no danger of starting a fire out in the desert, so we just went with it.

[*Sabrina S. Sutherland also weighs in on blowing up the cabin.*]

Sutherland: Patty Norris went to David and said, "Are you done with the cabin? Can I take it down now?" David didn't realize that her crew built the cabin and that we had to remove it when we were done. I remember Gary D'Amico didn't have the usual things to blow a building up. What he did was questionable, but we had a fire truck that came out from Baker. It wasn't even necessary because it was in the middle of the desert. There was nothing there. To explode the cabin, Gary put bags of kerosene in it. He was just trying to figure out a way to make something explode. If your jeans rubbed together and there was a spark, that house would have gone up. When it blew, the explosion was so beautiful *because* of the way it was set. It isn't something you usually see because it was not the way you rig a building to blow. Peter had set up the cameras and then everyone got out of the way because we had no idea how it was going to explode.

Ryan: How do you capture a live explosion that you can only shoot once?

Deming: I think that we certainly had the cabin lit for a couple of nights, so that wasn't really an issue. I was most concerned about not having the fire burn out or get too bright and lose its saturation. I was ready to turn the iris down on the cameras if that started to happen, but after the initial explosion, which wasn't that bright, it started to flame and burn with a lot of black smoke that was lit internally by the fire. I wasn't too worried because that was a perfect combination of fire and smoke tamping down the brightness of the fire, giving it the dimension and dynamic that you hope for. I don't know what the fuels were for this explosion, but it worked out photographically in a good way.

Ryan: It's a cool moment in the film. It's amazing that wasn't supposed to happen originally.

Deming: One of the three cameras we shot was shooting in reverse, so the reverse shot was not a post effect; it was something we shot in reverse on the day.

Ryan: What does that mean? How do you film something backwards? Is that the same technique used for The Red Room in *Twin Peaks*?

Deming: I didn't do any backwards Red Room shots, but I'd assume that's how they did it. Basically, you load the film in reverse and run the camera in reverse. David owns an old Mitchell camera that we used for some shots. It was really good running in reverse, so that's the camera we used to shoot in reverse.

Ryan: For Season 3 of *Twin Peaks*, you didn't film anything backwards?

Deming: No, because we shot that in digital, so it was much easier. It's a different story in film. I've done my share of backwards filming, so I wasn't sad to see that aspect of it go.

Ryan: The shot with Pete and Alice kissing is amazing. It is so dark, but it has just one small light showing their faces. How did you get that shot?

Deming: Initially the shot was them talking to each other, and the headlights were behind them. So we had the headlight effect coming from behind them with backlighting/side lighting—whatever we could get away with—for their dialogue. When they went to kiss, I was sort of concerned because that wasn't part of the plan. Watching them, the way the light was hitting them, and the wind blowing Patricia's hair and the dust really helped that shot survive, and that was one of those: "I'll be interested to see that in dailies," because there really wasn't a lot of light there, and I think that's a testament to the way we were exposing the film. The key light on them for a lot of that scene was them in the headlights, and they sort of whited out, and all the exposures on their body were six stops over what the lens was. There is a certain aspect of that when you are looking away but not to that extreme, and it's coming from behind them. I think whatever the light was hitting was sufficiently overexposed to not make the shot murky.

Ryan: When Patricia Arquette as Alice gets out of the cab in the silver dress, she looks incredible. Describe how you lit that shot in the garage.

Deming: That sort of sentiment of what she should look like combined with pulling up in a vehicle—which will notoriously show every light source you have—made us go with an almost commercial look, although much more contrasty than most commercials. I think for that whole scene, we had bigger and softer sources, double bounces, book lights, and things like that to give her that dreamy look that pulls Balthazar's character along to make him do unscrupulous things.

Ryan: On *Moonlighting*, to give Cybill Shepherd a Barbara Walters effect, they put a cloth over the lens. Did you use something like that?

Deming: We were using behind-the-lens nets for the entire film, so that was certainly a contribution to that. I don't think we added any diffusion glass on top of that, but that is certainly a fairly aggressive softening effect for close-ups.

Ryan: What did you have to do to film Alice versus Renee? Did you have a different lighting setup for the characters, or does it not get that specific for the DP?

Deming: It can get that specific. There was enough difference in her look and certainly when you add in what Patricia was doing with the characters. A certain aspect of it was whether they are the same person. You are constantly confusing these two stories, like the fact that Bill and Balthazar look completely different, but Patricia's characters are still Patricia. We didn't want to make it that different. There is the great device David uses with the photo in the mansion that the police find. You see it early with the two Patricias, and then later in the film, there is only one. It's a "which reality is real" sort of mentality. There was a certain value in keeping her looking somewhat similar outside the makeup, hair, and wardrobe changes.

Ryan: Speaking of which reality is real, do you have to understand the script to be the DP?

Deming: It helps to understand it. In terms of some of David's work—even now, there are questions after the film has been done for twenty-five years. Sometimes it's a heavy lift to understand it off the page. A lot of the first half of the film is a pretty straightforward mystery, so you certainly understand that. Other than that, you just sort of treat scenes as whatever mood they're in, whatever vibe they have, and feed off that. This is a long way of saying that no—you don't completely have to understand it. In this case, I definitely didn't completely understand everything. You trust the writer/director to tell the story and see the big picture, and that certainly has proven true with David.

Ryan: One of the shots I found interesting was when Mr. Eddy drives up the mountain in LA, and it looks like the shot is from a helicopter. How did this shot come to be?

Deming: It was done with a helicopter. It wasn't a big-budget movie, so we had a helicopter day where they did a bunch of aerial shots. It was almost an afterthought that it happened to be on that day. We just barely got that shot very late in the day. Fortunately, the camera was pointed down, so any daylight that remained was still working for us. I think David just likes terrain as part of the story. Certainly in that scene, it played into Mr. Eddy's conundrum with the tailgater.

Ryan: I love Patricia's eye shot where it almost looks like she is Batman. How did you get the light perfectly on her eyes and later her lips?

Deming: It was a pretty simple technique; we probably did a cutout on a piece of show card of foam cord or something and played around with that until it was the right size. I'm sure we probably set it up on the stand-in and made Patricia come in to make sure it worked. It was probably the same cutout for both the eyes and lips shots, just adjusted for each.

Ryan: Who makes that cutout? In Season 3 of *Twin Peaks* bonus features, you see that David loves to get in and make things himself. Did he make that?

Deming: No, I think we made that one.

Ryan: The first time I saw the film was on VHS, and the VHS transfer was horrible—maybe one of the worst ever. Why was my VHS copy so horrible?

Deming: I think a lot of the VHS copies were bootlegs. I don't even remember doing a video transfer master of the film. Ciby 2000, who financed the film, had probably, by the time it came out, gone belly-up, and it's taken so long for the 4K because there was a question of ownership or getting rights to the original negative. I'm not really privy to that, but that is the impression I got. Since it was an independently financed film from a bunch of different sources, it was almost like a "who's in charge" moment. I do have a laserdisc version that is pretty good. Other than that, all the VHS and DVDs have been crap until what is out now.

Ryan: Do you think it's the darkness that made other people struggle with the transfer?

Deming: I don't think it's the darkness. Certainly it's a problem if you don't have the original elements, and most of the VHS versions were made off a print somewhere, which can look good if you have the right equipment. They knew whatever version they made, people would buy. I don't think a lot of films have a lot of dark like that, and certainly to master VHS would have been challenging, even if you had the right elements, because the format couldn't really handle that much, which is sort of why the format has gone by the wayside.

Ryan: What is your favorite scene in *Lost Highway*? What are you really proud of?

Deming: It's hard to pick one. I really like the love scene in front of the car in the desert. I think that is a really interesting treatment for that. I like a lot of the early stuff in the house. We did this shot where Fred is searching the house, and she is waiting outside. It was

a shot of the front stairs, but the stairs are totally dark, and you feel the wall around it and part of the living room, and then the cameras are pushing in, and there is slow-motion smoke coming out of the blackness. That was sort of a "let's try this shot that David thought of in the moment," and it worked really well. Those are the kind of shots I really like.

There is a scene with Mr. Eddy where Patricia is forced into this room with all the men with a gun to her head, and I think this is a really visually striking scene.

Ryan: There are some major characters in this— you have Richard Pryor, Marilyn Manson, Robert Blake— any stories about interacting with any of these famous people?

Deming: Richard Pryor didn't really interact with the crew. We had him maybe for only twice as long as he was in the actual movie.

He wasn't hanging around the set much, but he was definitely an interesting character. The same thing with Marilyn Manson—we did those sort of blue movie scenes in prep, and again, it was a quick visit in and out for him. Robert Blake was around much more, and I remember during the party scene where he meets Bill Pullman, we were setting up the shot of his coverage. I decided to put a lower-key light on him to give him sort of a prominent eye light. I was standing on his mark looking at the lighting, and Mr. Blake is a little shorter than me, so I had my legs spread out to be his height. I was looking at the light and taking readings, and he came up to me from behind over my shoulder and just whispered in my ear, "Why are you standing that way?" I turned around, and he's dressed as the Mystery Man and all made up, and it was unnerving. I just sort of smiled and said, "No reason," or "OK, I'm ready, let's shoot."

Ryan: What do you remember about the atmosphere on the set?

Deming: During the love scene, the song that plays in the film was playing on set through speakers very loudly, just to get the cast and crew into the mood that David wanted for that scene. The same was true for Balthazar in those hotel hallways. That track from Rammstein— we had a huge speaker on the dolly, and it was blasting that song as we were tracking down the hallway, and the lightning machines were going off, and he's looking in these doors—the lighting and the musical soundtrack for both of those scenes was very specific. It really fed everyone—the dolly grip, Balthazar, the guys doing the lighting. Everyone could hear this track. It was guiding them, it was directing them. I thought that was really interesting.

The very last shot in the film, with Bill in the car at night, we were towing him in the middle of the desert in California in the middle of the night. We had a lot of lighting effects that required a lot of power; specifically, these carbon arcs we used for lighting, we had a lot of strobes. We had things hidden in the car—so we needed a big generator to accomplish the lighting that we had planned for the scene. There wasn't really a camera car, which is typically used to tow a vehicle, there were no generators to accomplish this, so we basically took the cab of the semitrailer that had two generators on it and put a deck on the back and towed the car with that. We put the lightning machine, the crew, and the camera on that deck. There were two cameras mounted on the car, and we proceeded to drive around the desert in the middle of the night with all these lighting effects going on. We were very focused on the scene, but then, later on, I thought about what a sight that would've been from a half a mile away on a different road, or from an airplane where you noticed it. It was this superbright source flashing in the desert, and I wished somehow that it was captured by someone.

Ryan: So you are the reason for all those X-Files cases called in that night?

Deming: I'm not aware of any UFO reports *from this.*

Ryan: Audiences were not ready for this movie, and the film didn't do that well. This was your first Lynch film—did you take that personally?

Deming: It didn't bother me too much. If you look at any of David's movies with the exception of maybe *Elephant Man*, they don't typically do that well at the box office right off the bat, but they eventually become cinema classics and are much more appreciated. This is actually a discussion I had with Sabrina Sutherland after doing *Twin Peaks: The Return*. It takes the world five or six years to catch up to the work that David does. It's very complex work and it is very challenging for the viewer, and it takes some time for it to sink in. You have to really steep yourself in the work to appreciate it. I was really proud of the film. I saw it with audiences in a few different theaters, and people really reacted to it. I think people just expect everything to be explained to them, and David doesn't do that. That's why I think critics find it frustrating. People become frustrated, but over time they appreciate what David has created.

CHAPTER 10
SCOTT RESSLER

When you've been covering the world of David Lynch for over a decade, nothing is more exciting than getting to talk with someone from the Lynch world who you never have before. During my interview with Sabrina Sutherland, she asked me if I had talked with Scott Ressler yet. I had to admit, I didn't know who he was. When she said that he was the first AC, I also had to admit that I didn't know what that was. I have since learned that means first assistant camera. As for what that job entails, I will let Scott Ressler explain in the interview. Besides running the camera, he is an observant creature on the set. He has worked on every major Lynch project since *Wild at Heart*. Not only does he run the camera, but he also takes his own pictures. He has a ton of photos from the sets of each film. He also listens and writes down fun quotes from the staff during the filming and then presents the photos and comments to the cast and crew at the end of the shoot. When I found out about this, you know I asked for a few of those pictures and quotes to be used in the book. Ressler, who now teaches cinematography at the University of North Carolina School of the Arts, was game, but David Lynch was not. Lynch declined the use of the photos or quotes to be used in the book.

Scott Ryan: How did David Lynch come into your life?

Scott Ressler: I grew up in Houston, Texas, and worked in a movie theater in high school. The theater showed *Eraserhead* as a midnight movie, so I probably saw it close to a dozen times because I kept bringing people to see it. Many years later, when I was a focus puller, some friends of mine worked as the camera team on *Wild at Heart.* I got a call asking if I wanted to be a camera assistant. I probably did around six days of work on it. My first day was at the Elk's Hotel in downtown Los Angeles. It was the sequence where Nicolas Cage banged someone's head on the ground, and I remember David saying something to the effect of "Oh, we need brains. Get me some ground beef." We all stood around as someone ran to the market and bought some ground beef. He mixed it up with some fake blood, or whatever his secret mixture was, and carefully placed it on the ground and the wall. I was thinking, "Every one of my idols that I've had the chance to work with has been a little bit disappointing, but here we are, and this exceeds *all* of my expectations." It was a really wonderful moment. I was just thrilled. Years later, I got a call from Peter Deming, and he said, "I have a movie." I said, "Let me find out if I'm available." He said, "It's with David Lynch." I said, "Oh yeah, I am available." That was *Lost Highway*, and after that, I did a long run of work with David. He was clearly my favorite director to work with.

Eraserhead was the Lynch film Ressler saw first; he then worked with the director for several years. Photo courtesy of Janis Films

Ryan: Describe your responsibilities as the first assistant camera.

Ressler: Originally, I was first assistant camera, and in England they refer to the position as focus puller. The way the hierarchy works in the camera department is director of photography, then camera operator, then first AC and second AC, and loader—at the time of *Lost Highway*, we were actually capturing things on film. The first AC is responsible for the camera equipment being prepped and ready on time, keeping everything in focus, and basically running the gear for the camera department. The second AC organizes the equipment and deals with paperwork. It's a tough job, especially the focus part and particularly tough when working in low-light levels, which is almost always the case on David Lynch films, so that was very challenging. David also has a unique take on focus.

Ryan: Others mentioned how David did not want things to really be in focus, especially the scene where Bill Pullman disappears down the hallway. What did David Lynch want that was different for *Lost Highway*?

Ressler: Interestingly, no one actually told me that David wanted to approach focus in a different way. I think they thought I would balk at that idea, so they just didn't mention it. On *Lost Highway*, we used E Series lenses, which are a type of anamorphic lens that Panavision made at the time. These are larger lenses—the previous series were called the C Series, which we couldn't get at the time. In this case, I believe they were T1.9 lenses, which means they could open up the aperture to fairly low light levels. That means that the depth to field, or the area in focus, is very narrow, and as a result, it's very difficult to pull focus. In the film days, where you were not looking at a high-resolution monitor to see if things were in focus, you waited until the next day to see if you did a good job with dailies. Apparently I did a good enough job, since I made it through the full film and he hired me again.

When we prepped this particular set of lenses at Panavision and tested them to see how good they were, we met with the head lens technician, Dan Sasaki, who is a bit of a legend. He found that they really weren't good at any distance closer than four feet. When David did push-in shots—where the camera dollied right up to the performer—he had the dolly grip, who I believe was Tim Collins, run the track right up to the feet of the performer, and I kept mentioning, "We can't get that close with these lenses." Tim would just shrug and say, "This is what they asked me to do." Every day I went up to David and told him that at some point the shot went out of focus, and every day he had a different response to that. One day it was "People are going to have to get used to a new kind of focus." Another day it was "I'll just add a buzzing sound to the soundtrack," and he did. So as soon as it starts to go out of focus, there is a really loud buzzing sound.

I found out years later that some people thought that we went out of focus accidentally on the movie, which was frustrating, since it reflects badly on me. Many focus pullers would have quit the movie because of how it reflects on me, since it makes it look like I wasn't doing my job correctly. But I wasn't going to quit on David Lynch. I was already a fan, and the experience of working on those films exceeded my expectations in so many ways. We actually had some input on David's sets; we could throw out ideas. It is absolutely David's film; he's not sitting there trying to decide what to do and looking for help, but we could throw out ideas now and then, especially if it is related to the technical craft. I wouldn't say it's a democracy by any means—it is absolutely David's creation.

Ryan: Try to go way back to 1995. It's easy to see why David went out of focus in retrospect because of the plot of the movie. But did you understand why he was doing it?

Ressler: I absolutely did not understand David's vision. I just had faith in it and did what was asked of me and tried to go beyond that. Watching *Eraserhead* as a kid, it was kind of an epiphany—it was another film that reinforced the idea that film could truly be art. I am the sort of person who will trust in artists once I've seen their work, even if I don't understand it. In a weird way, I'll respect it even more if it is more obtuse because I feel like they are taking more risks, which

Naomi Watts stars in *Mulholland Dr.*, but don't ask Scott Ressler for an explanation of the film. Photo courtesy of Universal Pictures

I respect. Except for maybe commercials, I've never really understood David's vision or would ask him while working on it. That is his domain. I still don't understand these movies, but I love them. I think how they make you feel is more important.

Ryan: Do you show your college students *Lost Highway* or *Mulholland Dr.*?

Ressler: Yes, absolutely. I suspect that David wouldn't want me to take things out of context, so we show the entire film. *Mulholland Dr.* has been shown several times. I volunteered to speak with those films, but so far no one has taken me up on it because I've said, "By the way, I can't speak to the meaning of the film at all." They're trying to analyze the film, so for someone to say "I can't talk about that" is not helpful to them.

Ryan: Let's talk about the hallway shot to get that darkness.

Ressler: I remember the way it was lit was unusual. We set up a tripod and made it as narrow as possible so Bill Pullman could get around the corner. We start with the camera looking into the room. He walks up into the hallway, where he's very close, and we pan with him as he walks in the hallway, and within a couple of steps he's into complete blackness. There wasn't anything particularly unusual with the first half of the shot, where he's in the bedroom. For the second half of the shot, Peter lit it in such a way that the light would drop off very quickly, and I had never seen anything lit quite that way without a second or third light to then take up the slack later. Then dailies came around, and as he went into the darkness, I had this intense experience, almost in my stomach, with a similar effect you'd get from a roller coaster. I was so shocked with how severe the drop-off was and how quickly he went into the darkness. I had what you may call a true David Lynch moment in dailies without any music or sound effects. Suddenly I got it. I immediately realized that this was what the effect was intended for, maybe not from an intellectual standpoint, but from a visceral standpoint, and I was just blown away. I could not believe how much it affected me—physically even. Skip to a few months later for a screening, I'm standing with Peter Deming, and the same effect happened in the theater. I remember a low gasp when that scene happened. Afterwards I'm standing with this group, and director Wim Wenders walked up to Peter and went on and on about that shot, and how amazing it was, and how much it affected him. I thought it was fascinating how we all had a common experience with this very simple, although well thought out and crafted, moment in the film.

Ryan: Tell me what lens whacking is.

Ressler: Lens whacking is a common term now, especially in the muralist camera world and smaller productions. It's an effect where you pull the lens out of the socket and shift it around to get an extreme out-of-focus effect. There's a related thing called free lensing where instead of moving the lens around, you let the sun or light hit the sensor to get a flare effect. Lens whacking is simply an extreme focus shift, like a crazy out-of-focus effect. You see it throughout *Lost Highway* and *Mulholland Dr*. It's become really well-known, but at least under that name, it started on *Lost Highway*. It began, I believe, in Balthazar Getty's character's bedroom. There was a discussion going on between David and Peter, and I heard the word "focus" mentioned, so I listened in. They were discussing how to get this extreme focus effect. I think Peter mentioned that if they just shifted the focus, then anything in the foreground would come into focus or the background, so it wouldn't really give him the effect that he wanted. There is a difference of opinion on how this discussion went down. I believe Peter remembers that he came up with the idea, David remembers that he came up with the idea, and I remember myself coming up with it.

Since I had done this before for a different effect, I just suggested pulling the lens out of the socket—this is how I remember it. Everyone's eyes got big and they said, "Oh, let's try that!" The reason why I had thought of it is because there is this old-school trick where you can pull the lens out of the socket and just hold it there to do macrofilming. Initially, what we were doing was have me loosen the Panavision mount and take the lens out very quickly but simply, and then just sort of shake it around. When Peter would tell me to, I would snap it back in and lock it in place. It was good, but the problem was that I couldn't see the image, so I couldn't see what I was doing and therefore it wasn't ideal. Peter further modified the technique so he

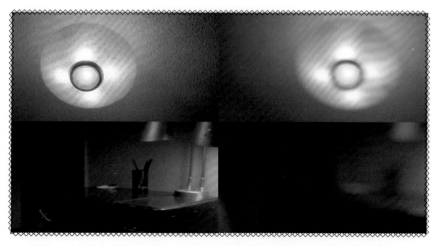

Here are two examples of lens whacking shot in Pete's room, where the technique was invented. First shot is in focus; second is blurred. Photos courtesy of Ciby 2000

could do it himself. We used the 75 mm lens, since it was smaller and used a short IP so Peter could get closer to the camera so he had more reach. Since it was an anamorphic lens, when you rotate it side to side, you get a really extreme distortion effect. That was basically the birth of lens whacking. I'm sure it was multiple people, but under that name that's how it came about. I don't remember if Peter or David named it, but from that moment forward, it became known as lens whacking.

Ryan: I can't think of when this was used in *Lost Highway* off the top of my head, but in *Mulholland Dr.*, was it used in the scene where Diane is pleasuring herself but can't get the job done?

Ressler: I'll never forget that scene as long as I live. It was one of the most painful scenes to film because we'd all become friends at that moment, and it was such a difficult scene for Naomi Watts. I know lens whacking was used more in *Lost Highway* than *Mulholland Dr.*, but I don't remember which specific scenes it is in. I know it was absolutely used in the point-of-view scene of Gary Busey in the yard in front of Balthazar Getty's character's house, and that leads to the Gary Busey story.

Ryan: Oh, Sabrina Sutherland did say this is a story we need to hear.

Ressler: We were doing a shot from a low angle, and the camera was on a hi-hat, which is a piece of wood with a tripod head mount on top so you can put the camera as low as possible. We are supposed to be Balthazar Getty's point of view, and the shot involves his parents running up and looking right into the lens and talking to him. The shot is in the front yard at night of their house. They asked me to do lens whacking during the shot, so I was sitting on a furniture pad on the lawn, low to the ground, while Peter Deming was operating. Gary Busey was in front and Pete's mom was behind, and as they ran up in the middle of the scene where Gary Busey was saying, "What's wrong with you?" I pulled the lens out of the socket and began turning it. I believe this is either the same day or next day that lens whacking had come into existence, so no one knew what it was up to this point. They say "cut" and then suddenly I felt my collar being grabbed, and Gary Busey was standing over me. He is a large man, and I was on the ground, and I believe his fist was cocked back while he was holding my collar screaming—well, maybe screaming is too extreme—but he was very strongly stating, "Why the hell are you changing lenses in the middle of my shot?" He was repeating this over and over again with a wild look in his eyes.

Comparison of the same scene with Busey and Gregson Wagner in focus and the scene with lens whacking, which Busey was not familiar with and not happy about. Photos courtesy of Ciby 2000

[Here is an insert from Debbie Zoller's interview]

Zoller: Gary got in his car and left the set. David and his assistant John Churchill had to jump in a car and go chase Gary Busey down the highway trying to get him back to set.

Ressler: It's not Gary's fault, because we didn't warn him that we were going to do this, so David ran up and grabbed him and with many reassurances walked him away and explained the whole thing to him. It really shook Gary and it really shook me, because it was a very imposing and shocking moment. From then on, I learned to warn actors. I don't mean to say anything bad against him; we took him by surprise, and it was a very emotional moment. There is a trust between actors and crew where they will support moments where they take a risk, where they go to emotional lengths, so to have someone do something extremely distracting while he was trying to give it his all certainly threw him.

Ryan: What can you tell me about filming with Rammstein as your soundtrack?

Ressler: Rammstein had sent a box of CDs to David Lynch, and he decided to use two of the songs in the movie. So they were predetermined and already in before the movie was even filmed. We actually played the song during the scenes to give some inspiration to Bill Pullman. They had a lightning box, an arch box, which is a big plexiglass box with a scissorlike mechanism holding two pieces of carbon. When you bring the two pieces of carbon together, they generate an immense amount of light. It was a common way of doing lightning effects on movies for many years. It draws so much power that you had to bring a separate generator. It was a really unusual way to film a scene. At the time, I had long hair and so did the gaffer, Michael LaViolette, and so while we were filming that scene, just to make David laugh while he was hiding in a little nook in the hallway, as we passed by, both Michael and I were headbanging to the music, and there was a lot of laughter from that.

Ryan: What was your part in burning down the cabin?

Ressler: It was sort of a last-minute decision, so production had to rush to get it all approved and legal, so it was unexpected. It was really beautiful to watch; it was insanely gorgeous. David owned an old movie camera called a Mitchell Mark II, and it was one of those Mickey Mouse ear magazines with the two circles on top of the camera, and you could film in reverse with that camera simply by putting the film in the other side and twisting the cable that was part of the pulley system from the motor to the magazine. We did that and filmed the whole scene in reverse, so it wasn't edited in reverse. I set up the camera so it was ready to film. I don't remember who operated the camera.

Ryan: That Death Valley hotel seems pretty creepy.

Ressler: The hotel had an area referred to as an opera house, and the people who had owned it had painted the interior as an audience in the theater. It was really unusual. It was known to be a haunted place. At one point, our Steadicam operator Dan Kneece said that he asked the owner about ghosts. The owner listed several ghosts who had been seen fairly regularly, and one of the ghosts was half of a cat. Somehow a cat had been chopped up, and half of it roamed the halls of the hotel, and that was the one that had been seen most often.

Ryan: Did you run the camera that captured the opening credit sequence?

Ressler: We were on an insert car, and Dan Kneece and I were on the hood of the car. Dan was holding his Steadicam. It was cold that night, and we were wrapped in a furniture pad as much as we could, but we had to work, so we couldn't be completely covered. We didn't film it at full speed; we undercranked it and ran the camera a little slower to increase the effect of moving fast. As a result, you have to roll for a lot longer because, for instance, if you film at six frames per second instead of twenty-four, you have to run four times longer to get the same length of shot, since it is rolling slower. I remember that each take was around ten to twenty minutes, so they were very long takes. I don't recall if the highway was a locked-off area, or it may have been a small highway that wasn't currently in use. While filming the shot, you couldn't really perceive the effect because we were driving slower, and we were freezing. We didn't really get it until dailies, and it was so beautiful. But the floatiness of it was because of the fine work of Dan on Steadicam.

Ryan: What was the Richard Pryor experience like?

Legendary comedian Richard Pryor, in his last film role, plays the garage manager, Arnie. Photo courtesy of Ciby 2000

Ressler: David just said to Richard, "Do whatever you want." I'm sure he directed him, but we just rolled and rolled and rolled on Richard Pryor. I was a huge fan, so it was just an unexpected joy. I didn't know he was going to be there that day, and I couldn't have been more thrilled. It was really an amazing moment.

Ryan: How was Patricia Arquette on the set?

Ressler: Patricia used to tease David. He is famously known for not wanting to be asked about what the *Eraserhead* baby was. Patricia got wind of that somehow and walked up on set and asked, "What is the *Eraserhead* baby, anyway?" She would also come onto set in the morning and say, "Good morning, Satan!" Patricia was amazing and was fantastic to work with. I've worked with her three or four times. On *The Hi-Lo Country*, I was walking back from a funeral scene and our paths sort of merged, and she said, "We've worked together before." I mentioned *Lost Highway*, and she just turned bright red and said, "The movie I got naked in!" And then ran off embarrassed. I think that was a somewhat traumatic experience for her.

Ryan: How do you look back at the legacy of *Lost Highway?*

Ressler: *Lost Highway* was a very important film for me. I had a few films that I worked on that changed the way I approached filmmaking and changed people's perception of me since I had worked on this amazing quality project. After *Barton Fink* and *Lost Highway*, I was able to get jobs that I would have never been considered for before. In that respect, it was fantastic. So few people saw *Lost Highway* upon first release that it was very disappointing, but I was just thrilled to have worked on this incredible project. Nothing could take that away. It was disappointing that it didn't make as big of an impact on the world at the time as it did on me, but since then I've met people who adored or even worshiped that film, so I think the long-term impact has been great, widespread, and significant. There was nothing disappointing about the experience, even the reaction to it. *Lost Highway* was a film where I had to put complete faith in the director in a way that had never been asked of me before, and where I was glad to do so. I just had no idea where anything really led. I would sort of step in these doorways without knowing where I was going, and it was a really fantastic ride.

On the following page is a photo of the cast and crew from the bowling alley scene. Photo courtesy of Scott Ressler

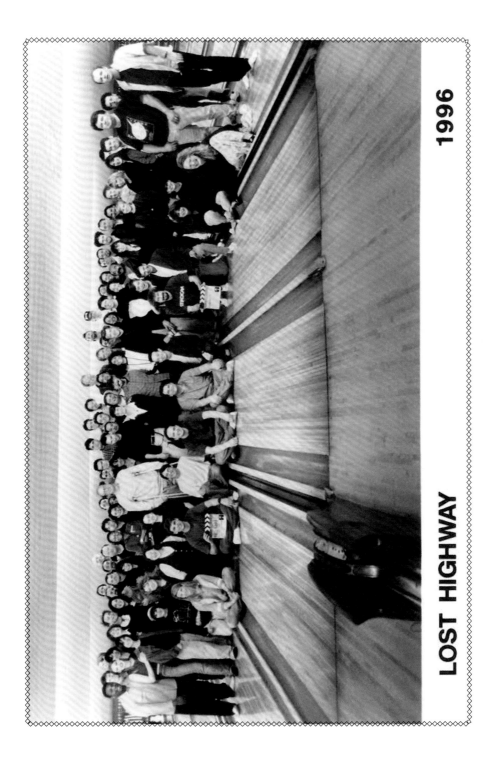

1996

LOST HIGHWAY

CHAPTER 11

NATASHA GREGSON WAGNER

I t doesn't happen very often. For me, it happens even less. But every once in a while, two people just start connecting and before you know it, they are dancing like Fred and Ginger, Uma and John, or Justin and Selena (depending on your age). When you meet someone for the first time, there is always that subtle dance that both partners do to keep their distance, to keep their balance, to keep their privacy. Natasha Gregson Wagner, who plays that girl next door Sheila in *Lost Highway*, is just as sweet, fun, and kind as her character. The two of us were talking and sharing within seconds. The interview that follows is just half our conversation. I am working on another project about movies from the nineties, so we also discussed her amazing work in *Two Girls and a Guy*, but I'll hold on to that portion for my next book. Gregson Wagner, as everyone who is anyone knows, is from a famous Hollywood family. Her mother was Natalie Wood (*West Side Story*), and her stepfather is Robert Wagner (*Hart to Hart*). She produced a wonderful documentary about her mother for HBO called *Natalie Wood: What Remains Behind*. I watched it the night before our call, and that might have led to me feeling like we were dance partners. Natasha Gregson Wagner does not believe in holding back. She puts everything out there and lets it fall where it may. It is that openness and complete honesty that make her a wonderful actress, and in my mind—as I do like to remember things my own way—my pretend best friend.

Scott Ryan: Where were you in your career before you got the part in *Lost Highway*?

Natasha Gregson Wagner: Before the film, my career was tragic. I had little parts in pilots that didn't get picked up. I was doing independent movies that weren't going anywhere. When my agent called and said, "David Lynch is interested in you." I was like, "Oh my God, this is a gift from the heavens." I went to his house to talk to him about the part, and he made me a cappuccino.

Ryan: Oh my, was the coffee good? It had to be good.

NGW: It was *so* GOOD. We talked about the part. He said, "Look, I don't have financing for this movie yet, but you are Shelia, so don't worry. As soon as I get financing, I will make you a proper offer." That is what I told my agents. They were skeptical, but he totally came through on his word. I remember I had been in Bulgaria doing this really bad movie called *Mind Ripper* with Giovanni Ribisi. It was just awful to be there. When we got back to LA, I was so happy to be home, and then I got the part in *Lost Highway*, and I had a nice little reunion with Giovanni. I already knew Balthazar from going out and stuff, so I was happy to be working with him.

Ryan: Did that help with the love scenes?

Natasha Gregson Wagner and Balthazar Getty knew each other before filming *Lost Highway*. Photo courtesy of Ciby 2000/Criterion

NGW: There was nudity in the movie. I felt insecure and embarrassed, but David was so sweet. He came into my room, and you had body makeup on you. He always had us use body makeup. So he was like, "Hi, Buttercup. This is how it's gonna be. It's gonna be like this and like this, and like this. It's gonna be a lot of fun." His tone and his matter-of-fact jolliness defused any kind of embarrassment I had at being a little bit naked. I had been in a movie called *Fast Love, Last Rites* where I had done nudity, so I was a little bit accustomed to it. I grew up in a household where we were all naked a lot, so I was used to it and not shy. But because it was David Lynch, and I was such a big fan and had seen all of his films, I was a little bit more shy than I would have been.

Ryan: What did you know about Lynch before the film?

NGW: I had seen *Twin Peaks*, *Wild at Heart*, and *Blue Velvet*. I was obsessed with him. It was seriously a shock when my agent said he was interested in me. I admired him for being a meditator and for his interest in dreams. I had so much regard for him. I wanted to do a good job. I didn't completely understand the script, and I told him that. He said I didn't need to—to just go with my interpretation of the script.

Ryan: Is it important to understand the script to craft your character?

NGW: I think you have to understand your character, and what they want, and what their function is. But I don't think you have to understand the whole of it. That is the thing about all art. Anyone who is watching—it gets filtered through their subconscious, and they take away what they want to take away from it. That is why I think the idea of critics feels unfair to me. They put an opinion in your mind before you have the blank slate to see the film yourself.

Ryan: This movie was really beaten up. How did you take it personally?

NGW: Yeah. I didn't care what the mainstream thought of it because

my experience was just so exciting. I wanted people to like it and for it to be well received, but I got to go to the premiere, and it was exciting, and to be a part of it. It didn't devastate me or anything. Also, I'm really just a supporting character in the film. It's really Patricia and Bill's film. I didn't take it personally.

Ryan: What did it do for your career?

NGW: I think it made people take me a little more seriously. I think it helped me get *Another Day in Paradise* and *Two Girls and a Guy*. I think the time between shooting it and it coming out was like a year, so my agents could talk about it, which let me get more auditions, perhaps.

Ryan: In all the characters you play, you are so full of spunk. Talking to you, I can see that is a big part of you. Do you try to bring that to your roles?

NGW: Genes are crazy. My daughter does so many things that remind me of myself. One of the things she has is that spunky quality. I didn't like that people would say in an audition, "She is a little too spunky for the role." I was like, "What does that mean?" Now I understand it. I was just born that way. I don't know, I just always have been spunky.

Ryan: There is a scene with Lynch directing you dancing with another young woman at a drive-in diner. It isn't in the film. What can you tell me about that?

NGW: It was supposed to be part of Balthazar's hallucination of me doing something against him. He didn't like that I was doing that. He broke up with me, but I didn't do the things that he thought I was doing. That was part of that idea.

Ryan: I don't want to hurt your feelings, but I don't think Sheila exists in the real world.

Natasha Gregson Wagner dances in a deleted scene from the diner.
Photo courtesy of Fine Cut Presentations

NGW: I think you are right. This morning, my daughter just did a presentation at school about dreams. They spoke to six different experts about dreams. The fourth graders were telling the parents about it. So me not existing makes a lot of sense based on what I learned today.

Ryan: Well, I'm not surprised that fourth graders hold the key to figuring out *Lost Highway*. But it does seem like you're really having a dream day today.

NGW: I am. Dreams are really fascinating. At lunch, David's trailer door would be shut, and he would always meditate during lunch. I thought that was interesting, and then I became a meditator. What's real and what's fantasy and what is a dream?

Ryan: This is another film of Lynch's that has strong female characters. Sheila is not a pushover. She is so strong.

NGW: No, not at all. Patricia's character too. They aren't pushovers. He really gave a voice to strong women.

Ryan: What is your best memory from *Lost Highway*?

NGW: I think the scene where we break up on the front lawn. David would come in and give a little bit of direction. I felt really held in his direction. I already had a friendship with Balthazar, so that was nice. It was a lot of night shooting, so that puts you in another dimension anyway. I mean hey, I was in a David Lynch movie. That is pretty cool.

Ryan: So I don't know how you will feel about this, but until three days ago, I didn't know you were Natalie Wood's daughter. You were always the girl from *Lost Highway* to me.

NGW: Oh my God. I love that. That makes me feel so good. Because I do think it got in my way as an actress. That is why I would like to act again, because I was able to process so much about my mom after making the documentary. I was able to put it out into the universe and let it go.

Ryan: The documentary flowed so naturally. When you ended up interviewing—if I could be permitted, can I call him "Daddy Wagner" like you do in the film?

Natasha Gregson Wagner and Robert Wagner talk about the death of Natalie Wood in *Natalie Wood: What Remains Behind*.
Photo courtesy of HBO Max

NGW: [Laughs.] Of course!

Ryan: Your interview with Daddy Wagner is just so heartbreaking. Do you mind talking about this?

NGW: Not at all. HBO said, "We are interested in making this documentary, but we want to make sure you don't shy away from the accident, so we want to see the interview with your dad first." The first day the interview wasn't going well. The director [Laurent Bouzereau] said, "We don't have it." That night, I said to my dad, "Listen, we need to go deeper. I know you like to talk about the great parts of your life with my mom, but we have to talk about what happened that night." The next morning, Scott, I am telling you, he was *right there*. He was so vulnerable. Laurent said, "What did you say to him last night?" But Daddy Wagner wanted to make this documentary, and I was so blown away by him that day.

Ryan: How did you not just cry uncontrollably during that interview?

NGW: Every time I did an interview, I didn't want my emotion to overtake the interviewee's emotion, but at the premiere at Sundance, when the movie ended, I just burst into tears in front of the entire audience.

Ryan: I was so moved by the honesty in your beautiful documentary. It's such an emotional look at losing a parent. My dad died before I became a published author. It has to be so hard for you that your mom never got to see you as an actress.

NGW: It is so true. I am sorry for your loss. It's so hard to lose a parent. You want them there to see your accomplishments. I do truly believe that they are watching. I spoke to this medium a few years ago. She said, "Hold up a piece of paper and just write what you want to tell your mom. She is closer than you think."

Ryan: Yeah, but wasn't it just Patricia Arquette who told you that? You know she just was an actress on the show *Medium*. She has no insight.

NGW: [Laughs.] That's true.

Ryan: I'm sorry for making a joke, it's what I do when things get emotional. Thanks for sharing all that with me. Why do you not act anymore?

NGW: I am married to an actor, and I tried acting when my daughter was seven months old. I did a movie that Tim Blake Nelson directed [*Anesthesia*], and I was just so miserable. I just didn't want to be there. I wanted to be with her. I am a hands-on mom. As much as you have to give to create a character, I just can't do it anymore. The way my brain works, I can't compartmentalize being away from her. I can't do it because most of me is always with her.

Ryan: That is nice, but I'd like to see you in stuff.

NGW: Ruth Gordon [*Harold and Maude*] was my godmother, and she won an Oscar when she was a much older lady. And I'm not saying I would win an Oscar, but I feel like she's an example that I can go back to acting anytime. I am interested in what I would bring to my work because I'm a totally different person now. I have more gravity to bring to my work.

Ryan: And then you'll go on your first audition and they'll say, "Ugh, she had a little too much spunk."

NGW: YES! "She's a little too old to have that much spunk." [Laughs.]

CHAPTER 12
BALTHAZAR GETTY

Balthazar Getty doesn't show up on screen until fifty minutes into *Lost Highway*, so it seemed fitting to place his interview later in the book. Before our interview, which was also one of the last interviews I conducted, I realized how many of the actors he had direct contact with who are no longer with us: Jack Nance, Richard Pryor, and Robert Loggia. It was then it really came into focus how much this movie is more Pete's than it is Fred's. Whom does Fred interact with outside of Renee and the Mystery Man? A bit with the cops, a scene with Andy, and a few moments at the end of the film with Dick Laurent. Bill Pullman's role is very solitary, but Getty's part is intertwined with so many other characters: Alice, Sheila, Mr. Eddy, Arnie, Andy, his group of friends, and his parents. Then I started thinking about the Mystery Man. To me, the Mystery Man has always been easy to explain. He was the true Fred. He was the evil that men do. But how does Pete interpret the Mystery Man? After studying the film for months, I was excited to think about that character only through the eyes of Pete. It made me realize how much work Balthazar Getty must have had to do to try to make certain portions of his section of the script, which runs sixty minutes, make sense to him as an actor.

It was truly enlightening to start thinking about the film from only Pete's perspective. All my theories and all the relationships of the characters start with Fred, because that is who we see first. This makes me want to start the film with Pete in the backyard, and then go back to the beginning once Fred shows up, then watch the end cabin sequence. Now *there* is a YouTube cut for someone to make. (Please don't do that. We never take final cut from Mr. Lynch.) The load that was put on Getty must have been a ton of weight to bear for someone who wasn't legally allowed to buy alcohol when filming started. Luckily, we don't have to wonder what that was like for an actor who had to carry a movie after it has been playing for almost an hour because Balthazar Getty was happy to tell us in this interview. Before we started talking about the film, he began our discussion with my favorite disclaimer that anyone has ever given me before an interview.

Balthazar Getty: I do want to start by saying we have stories in our minds and then we end up telling them, and sometimes I can't tell you if this actually happened or if this is a memory that was memorized and turned into a story, if you know what I mean.

Scott Ryan: I do. Have you ever seen the film *Six Degrees of Separation*?

Getty: Yeah.

Ryan: Stockard Channing gives a speech about that in the film. You should revisit it. She says we become "human jukeboxes—telling stories." I know exactly what you mean.

Getty: Sounds cool. The thing about being in a David Lynch film is everybody is a loyal student to him. They are willing to do anything to please him. He is so loved by his crew. I always feel like a soldier at his side. You always know you are in great hands.

Ryan: What blows me away is that you were only twenty years old when you started that film. Did you have any idea what you were getting into?

Getty: I was in a magazine. It was an editorial about me that David saw. He apparently fell in love with my look. He brought me in. I never actually read, and there was no auditioning. I just came in and spoke with him. It happened pretty quickly. I had been acting for a number of years and had a good reputation. David basically hired me on the spot. I knew *Wild at Heart*, which I loved. I have always been a massive Nic Cage fan—one of my favorites. I even tried to channel him in *Twin Peaks: The Return*—some of the physical stuff. I don't know that I was as aware as some people of the folklore of David and how beloved he is. I was definitely aware that I was playing opposite Patricia, who was already a family friend that I knew fairly well. I learned as we went through it why he was such a legend in the way that he directs. I was aware that I was working with a master.

Ryan: What did you think when you read the script?

Getty: You never got the sense that it was going to be as frightening as the film was. It was very hard to decipher. I could flip through it and see I wasn't in the first act. Initially there were a few days of rehearsals with just Patricia and I at David's house. Patricia's younger brother David Arquette [*Scream, Beautiful Girls*] is one of my best friends. She was a few years older than me, so she was like the older sister that everyone had a crush on.

Arquette and Getty worked on creating chemistry before filming.
Photo courtesy of Ciby 2000/Criterion

Ryan: How could you not. She's Alabama from *True Romance*. Everyone was in love with her.

Getty: Yeah. Me included. I was in awe of her. David was making us do some really intense stuff in rehearsals. Things like making us just look at one another—unbroken—unblinking into each other's eyes, which is difficult to do with anybody. It sort of broke our walls down. We had these really intense couple of days that lead into our first days of shooting. You don't know by reading the script what the film is going to be because so much of it was in David's head.

Ryan: When you are creating Pete, how interested are you in the Fred Madison part of the movie?

Getty: I never worried about the opening. The way we looked at it was the birth of Pete was in that jail cell. I didn't really look at anything before it. It was all to do with the fact that Pete was a child, then a toddler, then a teenager coming out of jail. David and I spent a lot of time listening to music. One of the ways I prepare as an actor is that I go through my script and attach specific songs to different scenes, and then I connect memories to those songs. Then I use those songs as a way to trigger the memories on the day.

Ryan: Wow, that is an interesting approach. Do you remember any of the songs you used in *Lost Highway*?

Getty: We were listening to a lot of weird African dubs. David is a huge music lover and musician, as am I. Lots of stuff would start with music. I would have something I would want to play him. We would sit in one of the cars and listen to it. One of the ways we communicated was through our love of music.

Ryan: What did you think of the Rammstein song?

Getty: I think it is so effective. I love Rammstein. David would do these amazing things where he would have big speakers on the set,

The soundtrack also got a rerelease in 2022 with a special vinyl.
Photo courtesy of Waxworks Records

so if there was a scene of walking at the beginning of the scene and no speaking till twenty seconds in, he would have the music on set blasting so you could hear what was going to be there. It allows you to get into this different world. I honestly think, and I am biased, the *Lost Highway* soundtrack has to be one of the best soundtracks to any film ever. David Bowie, Manson, Smashing Pumpkins, Trent, Lou Reed. I mean, it's insane. The fact that "I'm Deranged" is on there? Come on. It's such a special soundtrack.

Ryan: It's the only Lynch film that is filled with contemporary songs. You were twenty, so this should have been right in your wheelhouse.

Getty: I have always been a little bit of a hip-hop head. In those years, I was listening to a lot of Wu-Tang Clan and all of that great nineties hip-hop. But I have always been a huge Nine Inch Nails and Bowie fan. It was like fairy-tale actor stuff that you dream of but you never actually think you will get to do.

Ryan: Patricia Arquette talked a lot about how difficult it was for her to play Alice.

Getty: David had this specific way he wanted Trish to deliver her lines in an emotionless, deadpan way. I can remember times, after certain days, she would really feel like "What am I doing?" Feeling insecure in her own ways. Now we see it and she is brilliant in the film because David had this vision.

Ryan: How did you as an actor help her through that?

Getty: We already had this connection because of her brother, and then we became fast friends. I supported her in the way you support a best friend. "I am here to listen. I understand what you are saying." But I could see her performance on the monitor, and I'd tell her how incredible her performance was and how amazing this was going to be. But also, I understood where she was coming from and how explicit some of the scenes were for her to do. It isn't even about what you have to say, but just spending a lot of time in her trailer and listening to her. Both of us were very confused at times at the tone of the film. It has a very specific tone, and sometimes there will be a humorous moment and then it shifts the tone a little bit. It's hard as an actor to pin down what it is.

There is a scene I had early in the shoot that didn't make the cut of the film. Right after I get out of jail, my parents are giving me a sandwich. It is like a day after prison, and they are checking on me in the kitchen. It was a very small scene. We did one take. Then another take. Now it's five takes. Ten takes. I am starting to really feel insecure and thinking I am not good enough. Now it's fifteen takes. I am feeling completely gutted. This is not what you want on your first couple of days—to not be able to deliver on your first couple of days. David broke for lunch and said, "We will get it after lunch." You know that's not good. You normally work, have lunch, and after lunch you move on to something new. I went back to my trailer, and

I can remember crying. Then these are the stories that I don't know what is imagined or what is real, but some version of this happened. I got into my trailer, and after some time, somebody delivered a handwritten note from David to me. The note said, "When your mom gives you the sandwich, imagine that you will never grow old or never become ill. When you are speaking to your father, imagine there is a hummingbird on his head singing you a lullaby." I can remember taking that in, and it made sense to me. I came back after lunch, and we rolled cameras and got it in one take. That goes back to the idea that Pete was born in the jail. Lynch was trying to create an awe in my eyes that a child has when they see things for the first time.

Ryan: I love the idea that Pete is growing up.

Getty: Another big scene for me was in the scene when Patricia and I are in the hotel, and she is making the plan for me to kill Andy. I remember halfway through the scene, David put my hands under me, and he made me sit on my hands for that entire scene. Actors tend to use their hands a lot as a way to describe things. Forcing me to sit on my hands and go through that scene pushed me as an actor and made me focus on conveying things through my eyes and smaller gestures. There were always amazing lessons like that I carry through to this day.

Look Ma, no hands. Getty is sitting on his hands in this scene.
Photo courtesy of Ciby 2000

Ryan: Your character interacts with Sheila and Patricia. How did Pete view those women?

Getty: Natasha is a great friend of mine and is amazing in the movie. I think she was Pete's high school sweetheart and was a place to get out some of his sexuality. She sees the relationship as much more. When Pete sees Alice, it just hits him on a different soul level. Using the analogy of him growing up, if the jail is the birth, Natasha is the teen relationship and Patricia is the young-adult relationship—much more serious and willing to go to any lengths to have it.

Ryan: When Alice gets out of that cab, I'm not sure there has ever been a more beautiful person captured on film.

Getty: Agreed. That whole scene and them looking at each other, I can't think of another scene in a film where a young lady appears like that. I think every man, woman, and child is falling in love with that person.

Ryan: Was there pressure on you to act in that scene because we are looking towards Pete's reaction? There are no lines.

Getty: Like you said, it wasn't hard to look at her and be seduced by her beauty. I am actually the type of actor that feels comfortable when there aren't a lot of words. You convey it with a look. At the time, when we were shooting it, I couldn't have imagined how iconic that sequence would become. He is rolling slo-mo and doing things in post. He is doing multiple takes of everything, and he is so great at picking performances. The way I remember that is him saying, "She is getting out of the taxi and you guys are staring at each other lustfully," and that was it.

Ryan: If there is an iconic scene in *Lost Highway*, it is the tailgating scene. You were right there with a front-seat view of Robert Loggia.

Getty: I loved Loggia, and we had a great rapport. He was very much

A fan-favorite scene; Loggia lets his road rage roam.
Photo courtesy of Ciby 2000/Criterion

that character. It wasn't like he was one way—happy-go-lucky—and then we were rolling cameras and suddenly he was this menacing mob character. I remember him being one and the same. We had a lot of great scenes. I remember him grabbing me on the back of the neck or slapping me on the cheeks. I didn't want to be too buddy-buddy with him. It's easy when you are on set—you have all this downtime sitting on your chair, chatting away—and then suddenly you know they are a grandpa or this or that. I always wanted to keep a little bit of distance and respect for the performance. Then, being in the car with him, I can remember watching him flip out on that tailgater guy.

Ryan: Did you know the tailgating scene was going to be such an iconic scene? When I have watched *Lost Highway* with an audience, that scene plays like it's from an Adam Sandler comedy.

Getty: In post, Lynch sort of sped up the film—almost adding a silent film kind of tone to it. That adds a slapstick thing to it. I never got the sense it was going to be "funny" in that way. For me and the character, it was just another example that this is a very dangerous man, and you are sleeping with, dating, falling in love with his mistress. You should be fearful. I wasn't aware it was going to be a standout scene and make people laugh. I think a lot of that has to do with the fact that everybody hates a tailgater. [Laughs.] Where there are these universal truths, and we all identify with them, that is when audiences get to be involved.

Ryan: Tell me about Richard Pryor.

Getty: His disease had already progressed, so he wasn't where he was a few years earlier, but I took every chance I could to be next to him, to share words with him, being fully aware that this is the greatest comedian of alltime. I sort of hold that as a badge of honor that I shared screen time with him.

Ryan: Did he make you laugh?

Getty: He did. He would make jokes and still was quick as a whip.

Ryan: For longtime Lynch fans, the fact that this is Jack Nance's final performance is always bittersweet. You are the last actor to work with him. Do you have any Nance memories to share?

Getty: I wasn't fully aware of his history with David, and he was this alum. I just remember a kind, sweet, quiet intensity about him, a

Jack Nance's final Lynch performance
Photo courtesy of Ciby 2000/ Criterion

Red romances Shelly in *Twin Peaks: The Return*.
Photo courtesy of Showtime

niceness about him. We didn't get to have much screen time. Even in the movie, he has a couple of these great little moments that are unique to him. I look at it fondly.

Ryan: Well, he was in *Eraserhead* and *Twin Peaks*. While we are here, readers will want to know how you got cast to play Red in *Twin Peaks: The Return*.

Getty: I have always seen David as a mentor and someone I respect so much. David tends to use a lot of the same people over the years. We have always maintained a close relationship. I don't see him as much as I wish, but we are always cosmically connected. They just called me up and, per David, didn't tell me anything really. I didn't really know what the part was. They sent me a few lines here and there. No scripts were going out. It was super top secret. I had no idea what the trajectory of the character was, whether it was one line or multiple episodes. I went up to Seattle. Johanna Ray, who casts all of David's movies, asked me to come aboard.

Ryan: You might not have known what your character was before you started filming, but the question is: Did you know anything about

Red *after* you filmed it? Red was such a mysterious character.

Getty: Yeah, it was really fun. I hear fans seem to really like that role. I know there is a lot of speculation moving forward—if and when that happens—where would Red end up? It was fun getting back on set with David. We have a fun way of working. With digital, you can just sort of roll endlessly. With a lot of those scenes, we would keep the camera rolling, and I would go over to David, and he would give me some weird, interesting direction, and then I would go back in front of the actor, and the actor I was working with would have no idea what I was going to do. With some of those Red scenes, we would do twenty-plus takes—pretty much messing around. So the Red turn was a fun way to continue with David's story. We will always be connected.

Ryan: Back to *Lost Highway*, I have been told that a style of filming was invented with one of your scenes. They created lens whacking in Pete's bedroom. Other filmmakers started to use that, and it happened on your watch.

Getty: What is so crazy is all of the stuff that David and Mary Sweeney were doing is now all digital filters that create the same stuff. The stuff that they were doing in camera and in post have completely changed the game. There are so many different tools now to do this kind of stuff. No one is whacking lenses anymore, but there is a post effect to create that. When I see the movie, I don't feel it got the respect it deserved. There are so many things David was doing that I see to this day. He was so innovative, and they were difficult to do back then. Even stuff David Fincher has adapted in his work, I see the genesis of that being David.

Ryan: I agree. *Fight Club* is a great example of a style that comes from *Lost Highway*.

Getty: Yes, I feel like *Lost Highway* is the most linear film David has made. And the most commercial. That is why I think it got lost with some Lynch fans. I am not fully aware of the Lynch community, but I feel like it got lost between *Mulholland Dr.* and his earlier stuff. Maybe it wasn't weird enough for some of the die-hard Lynch fans. Do you know what I mean?

Ryan: Oh, I love what you are saying, because it is the subject of my introduction to this book.

Getty: I think it's the most beautiful film. It has this romantic love story. It is scary. It moves really well. The pacing is incredible. I don't think it got what it deserved in terms of David's body of work. For me, it is up there with the best of them. I know it's weird coming from me.

Ryan: No, I think you can have that opinion even if you are in it.

Getty: I have had a lot of incredible actors come up to me and say that is their favorite film. I have always been so flattered by my peers with huge careers who know the film, love it, and have Asian or German posters of the film. Maybe it's the least known in some circles, but then not a week goes by that I don't get a message from someone saying it's their favorite.

Ryan: Did you take the criticism personally?

Getty: I am still not aware of what they said. I know how I feel about the movie, and I have heard for twenty-five years the opposite of whatever the critics had to say. Look, you are writing a book about it, it's been restored, and people are still talking about it. That wouldn't be happening if people didn't care about it.

Ryan: How was shooting out there in the desert?

Getty: That was very early on. We shot the love scene with Patricia and I where we are nude in the desert where we become these white shining bodies. I had a lot of nerves about Patricia and I having to be completely nude in front of everyone. I do love the desert, and it set the tone of the film for everyone with these beautiful night shots in the desert. We spent a couple of weeks out there. We stayed in a place that I go to every couple of years called the Furnace Creek Inn. It was built in the twenties where mobsters that were on the lamb from Vegas would go to stay. I was out there a couple of years ago. We stayed there, and it was amazing. We also shot the scenes where I am looking in different doors at that hotel. Sometimes when I am not in a scene, I would hang out anyway. I remember they were shooting something in the cabin. David went back into the cabin and adjusted some very small thing that the camera couldn't even see in the corner. He was basically doing some set dressing, and it made me realize that every frame is something David has thought about and is aware of. It really set it into my brain that this was a master of his craft, and he was aware of it all.

Ryan: Any thoughts on the line that Alice delivers to you: "You'll never have me"?

Getty: That taps into Fred's insecurity and his obsession with this girl, and that he will never have that. A lot of that is about the infidelity that Fred is perceiving. Then it is the universal feeling of not being able to obtain something. Even when you say it, I can see and hear Patricia saying that line. It just sticks out as an image and a sound.

Ryan: Who is the Mystery Man from Pete's perspective?

Getty: Honestly, so much of that, the less you understood it—the better. There were times we would be reading scenes and say, "I don't understand this." You could almost allow yourself to become frustrated by that. Even now, certain things are like that. When you are mentioning the Mystery Man, I almost don't know what you are talking about. Certain mysteries will remain forever. There are so many things about the movie I don't understand, and I never will.

Ryan: I just have never thought about the Mystery Man from Pete's mindset before.

Getty: Yeah, that storyline kind of ties back to Fred. I have always seen it as almost two different movies. I didn't do any deep diving into Fred's part because it didn't pertain to Pete or give me any insight because Pete isn't aware of any of that. For me, the arc was just Pete's story, which can sit separately.

Ryan: If you could hang a frame from this film on your wall, what would it be?

Getty:

Photo courtesy of Peter Deming

CHAPTER 13
I'M DERANGED (REPRISE)
PART 1: JACK NANCE TRIBUTE

Embodying the sentiment of "There are no small parts, only small actors," Jack Nance may have had a small part, but he was never a small actor. He was always larger-than-life. Nance became David Lynch's first leading man when Lynch cast him as Henry Spencer in *Eraserhead*. Nance and Lynch became such good friends during the four years it took them to complete the film that Lynch used Nance in just about every film he created afterward. Jack Nance was not in *The Elephant Man* or the final cut of *Fire Walk With Me*, although he was in *The Missing Pieces* which are the deleted scenes from that film.

In addition to his appearance in so many Lynch projects, Nance's personal life intertwined with others from the Lynch universe. He was married to the late Catherine Coulson, who portrayed the Log Lady on *Twin Peaks*. He was roommates with his *Eraserhead* costar and future *Twin Peaks* cast member, Charlotte Stewart (Mary X, Betty Briggs).

Stewart told me in a recent interview, "I met Jack when we were doing *Eraserhead*. David Lynch was a student at the time, and I was just doing him a favor. I used to do student films because how else were they going to learn to make films unless they had professional actors to work with? We were shooting at the American Film Institute. The first scene I did was when Henry comes to dinner to meet my parents. We had a lot of downtime because David Lynch took forever to shoot. I thought, "This guy is never going to make it." [Laughs.] We were also working at night. He didn't start till eleven or twelve at night. There was just all this downtime. It was painful. Jack never talked. It wasn't like he talked about himself. He would just sit there. It was really hard to get to know him. I got to know his wife, Catherine Coulson, who most people know as the Log Lady from *Twin Peaks*. Catherine was there all the time. She is the one that created Henry's hairstyle."

The late Catherine Coulson told *The Quietus* in 2013 a little about her marriage to Jack Nance. She said, "We were married for eight years, half of which we spent on *Eraserhead*, and I think that became a distraction of sorts from the reality of what was going on in our personal lives. I truly loved that man, but alcoholism is a disease, and in the end the disease got in the way of our relationship."

Nance battled alcoholism his entire life. He would sober up for a bit, but always seemed to return to the bottle. Stewart said, "Jack was an alcoholic, and when he came back from doing *Blue Velvet*, Dennis Hopper took him to a recovery place. Jack had a really bad drinking problem. It was going to kill him. In *Blue Velvet*, he got so out of it. David conspired with Dennis to take him to this men's recovery place. That was when I got to him. I was sober then. I had gotten sober much earlier, so I called him up and said, "How are you doing?" He said, "I knew you'd find me." [She says this in a Jack Nance imitation voice and then laughs.] I invited him to come live at my house. My roommate had just moved out, and he had no place to go. He was pretty broke, so he moved in with me in the San Fernando Valley. We were not a couple; we were roommates. We invited David Lynch to dinner and had a nice reunion. He told us

Jack Nance as Pete Martell
Photo courtesy of CBS

he was developing a new show, and he wanted both of us to be in it. That was *Twin Peaks*. We were delighted. By that time, Jack was doing really well. He was staying sober. He was so much fun. He told great stories in that great voice of his."

Twin Peaks certainly made Jack Nance a household name once he delivered arguably the most famous line in the series, "She's dead. Wrapped in plastic" for over 34 million viewers on ABC on April 8, 1990. I reached out to both creators of *Twin Peaks* for quotes on Jack Nance and his portrayal of Pete Martell. One of them agreed to comment. Mark Frost said, "Jack was one of the most intuitive, instinctual actors I've ever worked with. He found a way to somehow disappear into every role he played while remaining indelibly himself. The gap between Jack and Pete grew so razor thin after two years. They seemed indistinguishable from one another. Everyone loved him. What a sweet, unassuming and swell guy he was."

In 2018, I interviewed actress Piper Laurie, who played Catherine Martell, Jack Nance's TV wife on *Twin Peaks*. During the series, the writers decided to trick the cast and home viewers by having Catherine Martell "die" in a fire. The actress secretly returned to the

That is Piper Laurie under all that makeup, but Jack Nance never knew it. Photo courtesy of CBS

series disguised as a Japanese man. To keep the twist a secret, Piper Laurie had to come to the set already in makeup. I asked her if Jack Nance knew it was her, and she told me, "Jack was an incredible human being. He was so naive, innocent, and dear. I was all done up as my Japanese businessman. There was great effort to not let anyone on the show know. Even my agents and my family didn't know—no one knew. My name was taken off the credits. Fumio Yamaguchi was replaced. I had done a number of scenes with Jack, and if he knew who I was under that heavy makeup, he didn't say anything. There was one time, he went to the producers and said, "Boy, that new actor is so weird." Then we did these scenes, nose to nose. I remember the scene at the bar where we were talking about musicals or something. We had this off-the-wall dialogue that was great fun to do. He was funny in it, and I think I was funny in it too. But he didn't know who I was. He didn't know! That was incredible. We used to have these parties every month or so; we'd have a party for the cast at a restaurant or a bar. At one of those parties, he got his script where my character reveals herself. He came up to me and pretended to be very angry with me. [Laughs.] He was very dear. A true innocent."

Charlotte Stewart seconded the label of "innocent" when it comes to describing Jack Nance's portrayal of Pete. She said, "In *Twin Peaks*, when you first see him, he is such an innocent. He is just going fishing and discovers the body, then later, when he is with Agent Cooper and he delivers the line "There's a fish in the percolator." Only Jack could deliver that line. You know Jack was also fabulous in *Wild at Heart*. He had a great scene talking about his dog. That was when we were sharing a house, and I went to the set and watched them shoot that. In *Dune*, Jack played a guard at the headquarters. All he did was stand at the door, and he was down there for a year and a half and hardly had a line. He was going to be *The Elephant Man*. David told him he would play the main role, but the studio wouldn't let him. I was also there when they shot *The Cowboy and the Frenchman*. Isabella Rossellini was there too. It was fun, and I knew a lot of the cast. There was Jack sitting on a fence post."

Jack Nance was a permanent fixture in the world of Lynch. His strange delivery made his lines seem more important. In *Lost Highway*, he basically only says, "I liked that." But every time I have seen the film with an audience, that line gets a laugh. He had a delivery that was singular. Think of him as Pete Martell saying "I feel like my lips were taped to the tailpipe of a bus." Or how he makes you picture his dog "Toto" in *Wild at Heart*. There are just some actors who can truly embody a line of dialogue. While Nance's life was lived as a celebrated cult-movie actor, his death was riddled with mystery. Richard Green, the magician from Lynch's *Mulholland Dr.*, produced a documentary about Nance's life and death called *I Don't Know Jack*. The film was screened in the spring of 2022 in Chicago at Daniel Knox's Lynch film festival at the Music Box Theatre where, I conducted a Q&A with Green after the screening.

Richard Green said, "My favorite moment in *I Don't Know Jack* is when Charlotte says, 'an unsolved homicide. Jack would have liked that.' And he would have. Jack was . . . he was Jack. I don't know anybody like Jack. Everyone we talked to knew him, loved him, and knew what a pain in the ass he was. And how tragic he was in some ways. You got that from every interview."

Charlotte Stewart explained more about the mysterious circumstances surrounding Nance's death and how it all started with

Friends and costars: Charlotte Stewart and Jack Nance at her 50th birthday party. Photo courtesy of Charlotte Stewart

the death of his wife. She said, "Jack met Kelly Van Dyke, who was Jerry Van Dyke's daughter. He loved her so much, but I think that was his downfall. They were fine for a while, but Kelly was an addict. He was on location for *Meatballs 4*. They were on the phone having an argument, and she said, "If you hang up on me, I'll kill myself." And there was an electrical storm going on and his phone went dead. He panicked and got a highway patrolman to drive him down the mountain to a police station where they called LA and had a policeman go to their place. She was dead. Imagine what that did to Jack. It was awful. He started drinking again and never really recovered."

After the death of his wife, Jack Nance struggled. He filmed *Lost Highway*, and then, just a few months later, he was dead. It is tragic for Lynch fans to think about what parts he might have had in the Lynch films that came after his death. One can certainly imagine him as a character whom Alvin Straight would have encountered in *The Straight Story*. Who would he have been in *Mulholland Dr.*? Would he have been a rabbit in *Inland Empire*? And how nice would it have been to see Pete Martell one more time in *The Return*? None of this was to happen because of a fight at a doughnut shop.

Former married couple "The Nances" attend a Milford wedding in *Twin Peaks*. Photo courtesy of CBS

Stewart explained what is known about Nance's curious ending. She said, "He was in Pasadena and rented a small apartment. Apparently, he got up in the middle of the night and went to a doughnut shop and got in a fight with a couple of guys. He mouthed off to them, like he often did, and they punched him, and he hit his head. The next day he was found dead in his apartment. He must have had a brain injury. It was a tragic end to his life. He was eccentric in the most fabulous way."

His assailants were never apprehended, and no one knows who threw the punch that led to the death of Jack Nance. On January 4, 1997, the *Los Angeles Times* reported, "Authorities said Friday that actor Jack Nance, star of the 1978 cult film *Eraserhead*, was struck during a fight a day before he was discovered dead in his South Pasadena home." The article went on to report, "The 53-year-old actor, whose full name was Marvin John Nance and who appeared in several David Lynch movies, was punched in the head during a fight with two men Sunday at a doughnut shop, said Deputy Mark Bailey of the Los Angeles County Sheriff Department. The two men were described as Latinos in their early 20s. Homicide detectives said Nance had blunt-force head injuries, but the cause of death has not been determined."

"'An unsolved homicide" became the final plot twist in a life full of ups and downs. Even with all the sadness surrounding his life and death, it is humor and warmth that his friends remember the most. Charlotte remembered just what it was like to room with Jack Nance.

Stewart said, "His room was a complete disaster. It had so much furniture in it. He had ashtrays everywhere. It was a mess. One day when he was out, I cleaned his room, did laundry, emptied all the ashtrays, and cleaned it all up. When he came home, he went into his room and yelled, 'I've been ROBBED!' [Laughs.] At Jack's funeral, I told the story about when I was on location filming *Tremors* and we were sharing a house. Jack was supposed to take care of the house. I came back six weeks later, and the lawn was like a foot high. I am sure the neighbors were really pissed off. I said, 'What happened?' He said, 'I lost the lawnmower.' That was Jack."

I liked that.

PART 2: ONE FOR THE ROAD

Movie lore says that Orson Welles's classic film *Citizen Kane* was almost set on fire by the studio instead of it being released to the public because it was so hated when it was first screened. Frank Capra's *It's a Wonderful Life* was a huge failure upon its release, and now it's a Christmas classic. Not every film is embraced during its initial run or even in the era it was released. That being said, I am pretty confident that *Lost Highway* isn't going to be played yearly on NBC prime time every Thanksgiving, but it has started to have the smallest bit of redemption in 2022. That can be evidenced in *Lost Highway*'s 4K rerelease to theaters, the Waxwork Records special-edition vinyl release of its soundtrack, and Criterion's Blu-ray release.

While Balthazar Getty was kind enough to mention that this book shows that people are interested in taking another look at the film, I am not as optimistic that this movie will have a true rebound in the way that *Fire Walk With Me* has over the past few years. It might be a little too soon to call it. I will always admit that as the managing editor of the Lynch-centric magazine *The Blue Rose*, I live inside a Lynch bubble where all his films seem to be Hollywood classics. There isn't a day when my Twitter or Instagram feed is not full of *Twin Peaks*, *Wild at Heart*, or Eraserhead quotes, pictures, or anniversary dates. Although, going back to my *Blue Rose* connection, I can say with sadness that our *Lost Highway* issue was the lowest-selling issue we ever did, so I am not sure that even Lynch fans are truly ready to give this film what it deserves. But after speaking with most of the cast and a good portion of the crew, what have we learned about the legacy of the film?

Similar to *Blue Velvet*, *Eraserhead*, and *Mulholland Dr.*, the genesis for *Lost Highway* came from Lynch's mind. The screenplay originated out of the trifecta of personal events for Lynch: the O. J. Simpson trial, the fact that a stranger told him, "Dick Laurent is dead," and his idea of receiving videotapes on the doorstep that came to him, according to *Room to Dream*, on the final day of shooting *Fire Walk With Me*. This is Lynch's movie. Yes, he cowrote it with Barry Gifford, and Gifford's contributions are as important to the script as Mark Frost's are to *Twin Peaks: The Return*, but just like *The Return*, the final cut of *Lost Highway* came from the mind of David Lynch. That means if you are a fan or scholar of his, this shouldn't be a film that is ignored, forgotten, or, worst of all, lost. It has to be considered as much as anything else he has done.

In the majority of Lynch films, he is ruminating on the dark concept of a woman in trouble. He then blends that darkness with the feel of the glossy blind ignorance of 1950s America. Critics and fans seem to love when he scores violent or drug-induced moments to the three part harmony of the music from his youth. *Blue Velvet, Mulholland Dr., Twin Peaks, Wild at Heart, Fire Walk With Me,* and *The Return* all have moments with fifties-esque chord progressions to display the feeling of innocence while being surrounded by violence toward women. *Lost Highway* has the violence towards women part, but those scenes are set to the sounds and feelings of late nineties alternative rock. There was no musical safe haven for the audience in *Lost Highway*. There was no Roy Orbison to protect the viewer; it was all Rammstein or Marilyn Manson. Possibly it was just too much for the average person. *Lost Highway* is another film about a damsel in distress. Renee Madison equals Laura Palmer equals Nikki Grace equals Lula Fortune equals Dorothy Vallens. But the main difference is this film never gives the viewer a break from the darkness—not aurally or visually. It is that exact reason why I love it. A story this dark shouldn't have a fun side plot. There are no scenes for viewers to find a safe haven with a crazy, comic subplots like Jingle Dale in *Wild at Heart* or the botched assassination in *Mulholland Dr.* Viewers are forced to maintain the brutal feelings of male dominance that Fred and Mr. Eddy represent.

One of the main differences is the blonde bombshell in this film isn't really a damsel at all. She is the one causing the trouble for Pete. Patricia Arquette, in my favorite quote in this entire book, said it all when she said, "It was the first time I got to play a *monster*. Even though it is a monster made up in someone's mind. It was the first time I got to play a bad person." Alice *is* a monster. That is not comfortable territory for American viewers. The blonde wasn't being victimized by the male lead; she was manipulating him. She was outsmarting Mr. Eddy. She was setting up Pete. American audiences, especially in the nineties, were accustomed to the blondes being weak and murdered. The most meta/subversive plot point in the entire film is that Alice doesn't exist. And in American culture, ain't that the truth. So does this film have a woman in trouble? Yes, but that woman is Renee, not Alice, and Renee's screen time is significantly less than Alice's. This could be one reason that this film never clicked with Lynch fans.

The second issue that I think viewers had with the film is that they just couldn't get past the fact that Bill Pullman disappeared after the first hour. We expected our movie stars to carry the entire film back when we had movie stars. Even though upon study and a second viewing, it should be pretty clear to anyone that Pete is a figure that only exists in Fred's imagination. But this was just too much

The two leads are one and the same. Photos courtesy of Ciby 2000

for viewers, and amazingly some critics, to figure out. Mary Sweeney, who edited the film and is now a professor at USC, said this isn't a struggle for her students any longer. In my interview with her for *Fire Walk With Me: Your Laura Disappeared*, she said, "When I show *Lost Highway* in a class I teach at USC, nonlinear things do not bother students now. So the fact that the character changes from Bill Pullman to Balthazar Getty and it becomes a different movie just doesn't faze audiences now. He was just ahead of the curve. It was a brilliant idea. And he was challenged a lot on that plot at the time." It is kind of quaint that critics in 1997 just couldn't get this switch, and college kids in the 2020s could. I opened the book with a quote from Gene Siskel, who was one of the preeminent critics of that era. In that same review he also said, "As a critic, I am all for seeing something I haven't seen before, *Lost Highway* has that quality, but it also is a film that makes very little sense, to me at least, so its violence pops out and seems empty headed." This quote backs up both of my theories. He saw only the violence, since there was no old-fashioned music from his youth to sooth him, and since it didn't make sense the first time, it

Here is the ad from 1997.
Photo courtesy of October Films

must be empty-headed. And before we let Siskel's cohost, Roger Ebert, off the hook, he concurred with Siskel, saying, "I feel just about the same way." The two critics famously gave the film two thumbs down, and then Lynch put that out as an ad, saying, "Two more reasons to see [the film]."

While I wasn't a film critic in 1997, I freely admit that I wasn't ready for *Lost Highway* when it first came out, but when I gave it my attention for the first true time in 2017, the film was a revelation to me. It is always hard for me to pick my favorite Lynch film; it changes like the seasons, just as it should. Nothing can top *Fire Walk With Me* for so many personal reasons, but from a pure Lynch-story perspective, I think *Lost Highway* is his strongest concept, story, production, artistry, and finished product. He knows what he wants to tell, and he never gets distracted by tangents or self-indulgence. Hopefully, more Lynch fans will take another look at the film, and it will start to screen around the country more now that there is a new print of the film.

I have always felt that something fundamentally changed in Lynch's style after filming *Wild at Heart*. It's so obvious to see the difference between his work in the pilot of *Twin Peaks* and then his directing of Episode 8, the Season Two premiere of *Twin Peaks*. In between, he directed *Wild at Heart*. (I know he also filmed Episode 2 during that time, but there were circumstances and budget constraints that didn't allow him to do much "directing" in that episode. Also, a quarter of that episode was taken from filming of the pilot.) Lynch's pacing in *Wild at Heart* is so brisk that it is hard to believe it is the same artist who directed *The Return*. *Fire Walk With Me*, *Lost Highway*, and then *The Straight Story*, were all made in the nineties, and are the bridge to the slow pacing in his work in the new millennium. I have no doubt that viewers struggled with the pacing in 1997, but in today's Lynch world, it feels right for the film. The mood created in the Madison house is conveyed more with sound and pacing than it is with dialogue. That is my kind of film—show me, don't tell me. But while the pacing in *Lost Highway* is more akin to Lynch's later filmmaking style, the film is still connected to his previous work because it is highly fused with plot. *Mulholland Dr.*, which technically was written in the nineties, is his last film that centers around plot. But even it didn't have enough plot for the ABC television network, which passed on what was then a television pilot because they thought the pacing was too slow. Tad Friend reported in *The New Yorker* magazine that Lynch had a call with ABC about pacing and said, "I think it's not slow, it's not boring. It's my pace." This was a pace he was developing in the late nineties and became entrenched with in *Inland Empire* and *The Return*.

When a director has a career that is as long as Lynch's—which spans forty years—that artist is obviously going to grow and change. To me, his career can be split in two parts, with *Eraserhead* through *Wild at Heart* being the first section and *Lost Highway* through *The Return* being the next. *Twin Peaks* and *Fire Walk With Me* sit in the middle, where his style has a bit of both and is hard to judge because there were so many other directors and writers who played a part in creating that world. But classifying Lynch films into nice boxes is pointless. The important point, as a Lynch fan, is that he was at the peak of his abilities while making *Lost Highway*. Pacing, story, respect for an audience's time, strangeness, soundtrack, directing, lighting, capturing performance—it is all there in *Lost Highway*. There it is safely tucked away in the middle of his career—seven years after the bright, hot spotlight of *Twin Peaks* and four years before the Oscar glow of *Mulholland Dr.*. I have no lofty goals that this book will move the film up the ladder of his filmography's legacy. Critics and fans will always remember Lynch for *Blue Velvet*, *Twin Peaks*, and *Eraserhead*, but I hope that the interviews that are contained in this book will honor the work and artistry that went into this singular movie. There are plenty of superhero stories out there, plenty of love stories, plenty of action movies; there is only one *Lost Highway*. For a moment in time, fans of avant-garde filmmaking got to travel that dark road, lit only by the yellow paint, placed there by those who want to keep us from crossing the line. Thankfully, Lynch never worries about that. Even when he gleefully crosses them, smiling with a look that says "I'm deranged."

Dick Laurent
is
Dead.

SPECIAL THANKS

There are so many people who came together to make this book a reality. I can't believe I was given the privilege of speaking with such amazing artists while working on this book. But it is also crazy that I have been able to do so many other books as well. I will never become jaded about this time in my life when I was able to create art for others to enjoy. Thank you.

Patricia Arquette was a dream interview that I never expected to get. I have loved *True Romance* for so long that the idea that I would speak with Alabama was just too crazy of a thought. After asking my second question to Patricia, we got disconnected, and it seemed like she hung up on me. When we were reconnected, she made a joke about being mad at me, and I knew we were going to have a wonderful interview. She even asked to see a copy of the book and a *Blue Rose* magazine. She was as delightful as I had always hoped. (Watch her in *Escape at Dannemora*; she is wonderful.)

Deepak Nayar is full of stories. I am bummed he wasn't in my *Fire Walk With Me* book, but those stories live on in this book. The idea that he went from driver to producer seems like his life story should be a Netflix series.

Sabrina S. Sutherland has been so supportive of every Lynch project I have worked on. She is so professional, kind, smart, and nice. She is probably the person I have interviewed the most, and each time is a revelation. I am a big fan of hers, and I like to pretend she is one of mine.

Debbie Zoller's work is always astounding. She has worked on so many famous projects it is incredible. I met her in London at a *Twin Peaks* event and asked her if I could interview her, and she seemed shocked. I don't think she realizes how important her work is to the Lynch world, but I sure do.

Peter Deming sent me so many pictures, and because he is a photographer himself, he worried about the quality of them. That was refreshing. His work on this film is topped only by his work on *The Return*. I could have talked to him forever about that series, and some day I hope to.

Scott Ressler was so nice to offer up a ton of photos and quotes from the *Lost Highway* set. Unfortunately, David Lynch said no to all that, but isn't the offer nice enough? No, the pictures would have been pretty cool to capture for history. He has filmed so many amazing scenes in the Lynch world. It was great to talk to him about lens whacking just so I could say that phrase.

Natasha Gregson Wagner and I should be best friends. I think it could happen someday. My wife listened to the interview and agreed. I have loved her work since *Two Girls and a Guy*. You can read more of our interview in my upcoming book about nineties films. Call me, Natasha. Let's be BFFs.

Balthazar Getty and I became quick text buddies. He was very busy while I was prepping the book, but he made sure he had time for the interview. His love for this film is just what fans want to see from an actor. I am kicking myself I forgot to ask him about *Alias*.

Charlotte Stewart has never said no to me. She is such a dear friend of our family. She actually is as nice as she seems. I love her dearly.

David Lynch creates films that makes writing a book so easy because there is just so much to discuss. I am thankful he gave several interviews to other people about this topic so I could quote him.

Barry Gifford has written so many wonderful books and movie scripts. It was an honor to cover his work.

Angelo Badalamenti passed away two days before this book went to print. It's strange to think when I was working on the soundtrack chapter I was emailing him questions, and now he is gone before the book will see daylight. I have a real indication his music will light the way for listeners for years to come.

Duwayne Dunham is the best person to sit next to when you watch *Blue Velvet*. I was happy to use a quote from our interview at a *Blue Velvet* screening in Chicago.

Mark Frost may not have had anything to do with *Lost Highway*, but he was the first person to send me a quote for the Jack Nance tribute and is one of the most moral, kindest writers that I know. We need more of him in this world of egos.

Richard Green isn't just the magician; he brings magic to every conversation. My wife and I had a wonderful lunch with him in Chicago. His friendship truly matters to me.

A moment of silence for *Catherine Coulson* and *Jack Nance*.

Steven Miller is a prince of a man. He let me borrow his script of *Lost Highway* so I could do the compare and contrast. He also is a good person to sit next to when you see *Lost Highway*. We saw the 4K restoration in Orlando.

Glenn Gordon Caron is the reason I am a writer and the reason there is this book. He so generously contacted Patricia Arquette for me. They worked together on *Medium*. If you want to know more about him, check out my book on *Moonlighting*.

Daniel Knox made a lot of my dreams come true by allowing me to host the Q&As at his Chicago Lynch event. He also is a Lynch encyclopedia and a great person to be able to text when you are working on a project like this.

Ben Durant loves *Lost Highway* more than anyone I know. He was a big cheerleader for this book and always is so supportive. Check out his podcast *Twin Peaks Unwrapped* for more coverage.

Bryon Kozaczka really didn't do a damn thing to help with this book, but he is the other *Twin Peaks Unwrapped* host, so I felt I should thank him.

Courtenay Stallings is my favorite of all the Lynch scholars, and that includes me. Meeting her has changed my life in so many wonderful ways. She wrote a wonderful essay about *Lost Highway* for Issue 17 of *The Blue Rose* that I can finally read now. She is my family.

Mel Reynolds's support is just what a fellow artist needs when you are working on a project like this. I knew her before she was famous.

Mike Chisholm supports me for a very strange reason that I don't know. But he is a super great guy.

Brian "Dugpa" Kursar pointed me in the right direction to get some *Lost Highway* photos for this book. His dedication to the world of Lynch is unsurpassed.

Emily Marinelli is what a genie would bring to someone who wished for the best best friend in the world. Now I feel bad that instead I asked the genie for Babs to do a Sondheim album. Oh well, she kinda likes me anyway. Listen to her *Twin Peaks Tattoo* podcast. It is good. She is better.

Melanie Mullen must be thanked or she will throw this book away. I secretly love Melanie but would rather die than tell her, plus it would kill her if I told her.

Brad Dukes wrote a wonderful article about the soundtrack that I luckily read after I wrote my chapter on the music. Brad is always an inspiration to me and my work.

Thanks to the Sarasota Post Office. Special thanks to *Sara* and *David* who always help me out. (My true love will always be *Shameeka* back in Ohio.)

Mindy Fortune gets a big thanks for being my longest and therefore my oldest active friend. See, someone can stand me for more than a few years. Thanks for all the support.

Josh Minton is like a brother to me, but his wife is not like a sister to me. Thanks for all the support and kind words over the years.

Faye Murman and her drive-in event kicked off this book in high gear. Also, thanks for the author photo and the fun text messages.

David Bushman is the best business partner anyone could have. I am happy to work with him everyday. I missed arguing with him on this book.

Alex Ryan worked his fingers off on this book. He took his editing job seriously, and that made the book a better book. I am lucky to have a great son. My parents never had one.

Joyce Ryan is always there to listen to my crazy day. Thanks to my mom for the all the phone calls and supporting all my interviews.

Lisa Hession taught me what it means to be loved back when I was deaf from the Canton noise. How either of us can still hear is a miracle. I love you like we are still in the convertible.

Matt Zoller Seitz wrote a wonderful foreword and supports my business for some crazy reason. Please support his website: mzs.press.

Jen Ryan is the reason I am not wandering my own lost highway. Her love and support can make anyone get a book completed. I am lucky to have such a perfect and loving wife. We have had fun every day since we met. Few married people can say that, including her.

Thanks to everyone who preordered this book and supported each and every one of my projects. I never thought that this would be my life. I am truly thankful for each of you.

Before you go, I want to pitch you my religion. It's called kindness. Every day, I am confronted with a stranger's anger. It would always be easy to give anger back. I don't do it. I implore you to resist as well. Today, let a stranger be wrong and say nothing about it. Be concerned with yourself and move on with kindness in your heart. If each of us, one by one, put only positivity first, we can make the difference we so want to see. Charlotte Stewart's kindness to me is amazing. That Mark Frost, Piper Laurie, and Richard Green wanted to say nice things about Jack Nance is all we need to know. Don't focus on the ones that say no. Bring kindness to the world. The patrons at the post office and strangers on social media will try to make me be mean to them. I won't crack and neither will you. Be kind and love each other. Just do it quietly and without reward. If you have kind words about the book, feel free to email me at Superted455@gmail.com

If you enjoyed this book, post it on your social media and tag @scottluckstory or @bluerosemag1.

MORE TO READ ABOUT DAVID LYNCH

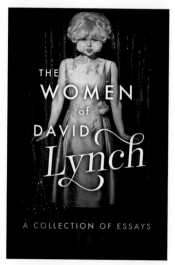

MORE TO READ FROM SCOTT RYAN

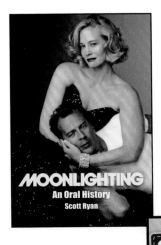

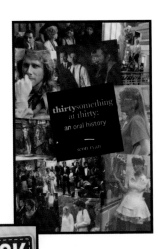

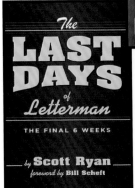

ORDER AT TUCKERDSPRESS.COM

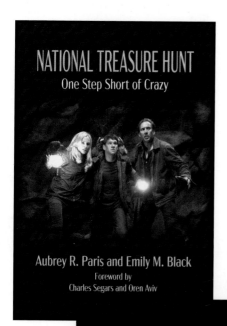
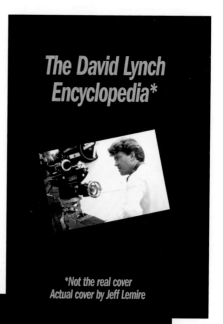